Cambridge Elements

Elements in Politics and Society in Latin America
edited by
Maria Victoria Murillo
Columbia University
Juan Pablo Luna
The Pontifical Catholic University of Chile
Andrew Schrank
Brown University

LOW-COST FASHION

The Political Economy of Garment Production and Distribution in Latin America

Matías Dewey
University of St. Gallen

André Vereta-Nahoum
University of Sao Paulo

Shaftesbury Road, Cambridge CB2 8EA, United Kingdom

One Liberty Plaza, 20th Floor, New York, NY 10006, USA

477 Williamstown Road, Port Melbourne, VIC 3207, Australia

314–321, 3rd Floor, Plot 3, Splendor Forum, Jasola District Centre,
New Delhi – 110025, India

103 Penang Road, #05–06/07, Visioncrest Commercial, Singapore 238467

Cambridge University Press is part of Cambridge University Press & Assessment,
a department of the University of Cambridge.

We share the University's mission to contribute to society through the pursuit of
education, learning and research at the highest international levels of excellence.

www.cambridge.org
Information on this title: www.cambridge.org/9781009634106

DOI: 10.1017/9781009634144

© Matías Dewey and André Vereta-Nahoum 2025

This publication is in copyright. Subject to statutory exception and to the provisions of
relevant collective licensing agreements, with the exception of the Creative Commons
version the link for which is provided below, no reproduction of any part may take
place without the written permission of Cambridge University Press & Assessment.

An online version of this work is published at doi.org/10.1017/9781009634144 under
a Creative Commons Open Access license CC-BY-NC 4.0 which permits re-use, distribution and reproduction in any medium for non-commercial purposes providing
appropriate credit to the original work is given and any changes made are indicated.
To view a copy of this license visit https://creativecommons.org/licenses/by-nc/4.0

When citing this work, please include a reference to the DOI 10.1017/9781009634144

First published 2025

A catalogue record for this publication is available from the British Library

ISBN 978-1-009-63410-6 Hardback
ISBN 978-1-009-63415-1 Paperback
ISSN 2515-5253 (online)
ISSN 2515-5245 (print)

Cambridge University Press & Assessment has no responsibility for the persistence
or accuracy of URLs for external or third-party internet websites referred to in this
publication and does not guarantee that any content on such websites is, or will
remain, accurate or appropriate.

Low-Cost Fashion

The Political Economy of Garment Production and Distribution in Latin America

Elements in Politics and Society in Latin America

DOI: 10.1017/9781009634144
First published online: January 2025

Matías Dewey
University of St. Gallen

André Vereta-Nahoum
University of Sao Paulo

Author for correspondence: Matías Dewey, matias.dewey@unisg.ch

Abstract: The literature on the garment industry in Latin America refers almost exclusively to the cases of Central America and Mexico, which are part of global value chains. This Element analyses a fundamentally new regional configuration of the garment sector, covering much of South America. Based on ethnographic fieldwork and in-depth interviews with a wide range of actors, it examines two major circuits of informal production and distribution of affordable garments, both of which have emerged around the urban marketplaces of La Salada (Buenos Aires) and Feira da Madrugada (São Paulo). This Element examines a configuration characterized by (1) manufacturers who interact with customer preferences to produce low-cost fashion, (2) marketplaces that function as large garment distribution hubs, and (3) extensive distribution routes with regional reach. This Element discusses the role of creativity in informal production processes, reflects on the implications of both cases for our understanding of global value chains and informality, and provides empirical evidence on forbearance as an explanatory element for the emergence of this phenomenon. This title is also available as Open Access on Cambridge Core.

Keywords: fast fashion, marketplaces, informality, Latin America, forbearance

© Matías Dewey and André Vereta-Nahoum 2025

ISBNs: 9781009634106 (HB), 9781009634151 (PB), 9781009634144 (OC)
ISSNs: 2515-5253 (online), 2515-5245 (print)

Contents

1 Introduction

More than 2,000 kilometers (1,242 miles) separate La Salada, on the outskirts of Buenos Aires, from Feira da Madrugada, in central São Paulo. Yet, a first-time visitor will encounter a strikingly similar scene: early in the day, the streets are populated by thousands of people carrying stacks of clothing items in carts to their selling posts or pulling large bags and trolleys where they place their purchases. In spacious warehouses and buildings, people gather in small commercial stalls to trade low-cost garments. Alongside or beneath the buildings, numerous parking lots are filled with buses. Most of the buyers in these marketplaces arrive by bus and return to their hometowns, distributing this unique form of fashion throughout Argentina and Brazil. The clothes sold in La Salada and Feira da Madrugada are primarily made locally in workshops located within the marketplaces, a few blocks away, or in other areas of the cities. We call this *low-cost fashion* because they are produced by monitoring trends in media and digital social networks and then daily testing pieces with their consumers. Although sometimes based on models developed by fashion retailers in South America or elsewhere, they are creative translations of what influential celebrities are using or niche clothes to publics like "plus-size" and "Evangelical" catering to the lower and middle strata in the income distribution. What differentiates this from fast fashion are the significantly lower prices and the distinct aesthetic and symbolic forms that resonate with these social strata.

In sum, they comprise regional circuits of production, trade, and distribution of low-cost fashion. This Element investigates these circuits to explain the causes underlying their development amid increased international competition and globalization of the garment industry. These marketplaces and their circuits have provided producers with the opportunity to produce directly for sale near their workshops, replacing contracts with international fashion retailers.

Leo's trajectory aptly illustrates the underlying socioeconomic dynamics of these circuits. Leo, a Bolivian immigrant who moved to Argentina in the late 1990s, lost his formal job in 2000. In 2001, he began manufacturing children's clothes from discarded fabrics and selling them at the La Salada marketplace in a disadvantaged suburb of the *conurbano bonaerense* (the Buenos Aires metropolitan area). Leo was inexperienced in manufacturing clothes but learned and perfected his business over time. He bought his first sewing machine with $50.00 his mother lent him when the Argentine peso was still worth one dollar. Over the next two decades, Leo progressed and channeled all his production through La Salada. Still today, this marketplace brings together some 8,000 garment producers like Leo and thousands of buyers from all over the country three days a week. In 2024, Leo has sixteen employees, two workshops, and produces 10,000 children's caps monthly. From a socio-legal point of view, Leo's workshops are informal: none of his employees is formally registered, several taxes are evaded, and none of the facilities used as workshops, which house industrial machinery, are authorized.

For producers like Leo or his counterparts in Brazil's Feira da Madrugada, the La Salada marketplace is the heart of their business. Leo has his stall, which he regularly rents to display what he has created in his workshops. For him, meeting face-to-face with regular or potential buyers allows him to "take the pulse" of what is being sold – and what not -, to check visitors' preferences, and to observe what other producers are selling. Both La Salada and Feira da Madrugada are the sites where producers like Leo sell wholesale garments to traders who come from far away. These wholesalers are fundamental. On the one hand, they are the ones who transport and resell to end users in distant places. These marketplaces also offer traders the opportunity to obtain income reselling low-cost clothing that embodies specific symbolic forms appealing to regional consumers. On the other hand, because of their strategic position between producers and end users, wholesalers are crucial actors in the diffusion of "what is in fashion." They collect information about buyers' preferences and share it with producers, so the latter can adapt production to new trends. It is based on these face-to-face meetings at the marketplace that producers make decisions about the garments they will manufacture for the coming seasons.

La Salada and Feira da Madrugada are classical marketplaces: their functioning is based on face-to-face encounters; personal relationships are crucial; there is informality in almost all aspects; the employees of the workshops are mostly family members; and the scope of this economy is not global but national or regional. Their recent development and endurance challenge mainstream trends of the garment sector in our time. On the one hand, La Salada and Feira da Madrugada are not digital platforms, and although the use of these instruments is not alien, there is a clear preference and need for personal encounters in the production and distribution stages. On the other hand, producers like Leo do not have a workshop dedicated to cut-and-sew operations of garments designed by others in charge of the "knowledge work," but their work depends on their ability to be creative and interpret clients' preferences.

This Element draws the reader into a phenomenon familiar to millions of garment consumers in Latin America, especially in Argentina and Brazil, but rare in the literature on garment production and distribution in the region. By focusing on companies – multinational or local – engaged in subcontracting, most available studies have neglected to examine marketplaces as central actors in this economic constellation. This Element shows the relevance of market-places, no longer as relics of the past that still serve a function, but as a specific format of business organization that is re-emerging: in relation to problems such as access to garments, to particular relationships with governments and state structures, and to the influence of specific symbols that comprise this low-cost form of fashion that is locally called "modinha."

These features distance them from the classic perspectives on marketplaces as "picturesque features of Latin American commercial activity" (Bromley and Symanski 1974: 3). Neither La Salada nor Feira da Madrugada is an ethnic enclave in the strict sense. Contrary to previous observations (Benencia and Canevaro 2017; Sassen 2011), this Element underscores the complexity of the phenomenon, which lies precisely in the fact that they are broad assemblages composed of migrants from different countries and different local actors. They are also marketplaces – and an economic circuit – that do not emerge as a self-organized commercial sector or as a post-neoliberal mode of protest detached from the state and linked to the effects of global capitalist forces (D'Angiolillo et al. 2010; Forment 2015; Gago 2012; Hu 2012; Pogliaghi 2008; Sassen 2011). As we argue toward the end of the text when discussing the perspective of global value chains, the low-cost garment circuits analyzed in this Element is largely explained by local or regional forces that reorganize, reinforce, and recreate global trends.

In this Element, we argue that the production, distribution, and trade circuits around La Salada and Feira da Madrugada emerge as a consequence of (1) a demand for garments based on the problematic access to garments sold in traditional formal shops, which represents a structure of opportunities for entrepreneurs willing to develop businesses in the fast fashion sector, (2) government and state institutions that, in the face of massive informality, respond to this new configuration by practicing regulatory forbearance (Dewey 2018a, 2020a, 2022; Holland 2017). The key structural determinant is the demand for low-cost garments and fashion products, and this demand is directly related to the difficulty of accessing premium brand clothing or clothing sold in malls or official stores. As we will show, La Salada or Feira da Madrugada are centered on the fast-fashion business which, similar to business models such as Inditex (Crofton and Dopico 2007), is characterized by providing quick responses to customer demands at low prices. To do this, informal entrepreneurs incorporate design into the production process and strongly focus on gathering information about customer preferences.

This business model and production process is not much different from what we know as fast fashion. However, the term "low-cost fashion" used in this research highlights price as a fundamental characteristic of this type of garment. The latter must be affordable, even if this means reducing the investment in the design and quality of the garments. The crucial importance of price stems from the mentioned lack of access to garments sold in traditional stores: this is the structural nature of the opportunities for garment producers in Argentina and Brazil. Low prices are also the result of massive informality at both the production and commercialization stages, much of which manifests itself in tax evasion. Through extensive regional distribution networks, these marketplaces offer opportunities for consumers of limited means, who would otherwise be excluded from the market, to purchase clothes they consider fashionable.

Second, La Salada and Feira da Madrugada emerge thanks to a set of actors who take advantage of the aforementioned structural opportunity which, as already indicated, is none other than the lack of access to garments sold in traditional circuits. In the sphere of production, the main emerging actor is the entrepreneur or garment manufacturer. Following existing work at the intersection of entrepreneurship and informality, we understand the entrepreneur as "someone who is actively engaged in setting up a business or is the owner/ manager of a business that is less than thirty-six months old, who is engaged in a socially legitimate, paid activity that is legal in all respects except that it is not declared to, hidden from, or registered with the authorities for tax, social security and/or labor purposes, when it should be declared. Therefore, the only illegitimate feature of the activity of these entrepreneurs is that some or all of their paid activity is not declared to the authorities when it should be declared" (Williams 2017: 7). In line with previous work (Dewey 2020a), this definition emphasizes that informality is basically interpreted as widespread non-compliance with various regulations, that is, taxes, licenses, permits, labor contracts, and so on. Although we do not exclude ideal characteristics of the entrepreneur, such as the desire for autonomy (Milanés 2024), we emphasize the lived characteristics of the work of this emerging actor, as they are what explain how it is possible to exploit the opportunities they encounter. Likewise, the entrepreneur does not establish any garment business, but of garments in fashion. Therefore, the entrepreneur's work is nourished by a constant flow of information that comes from monitoring the preferences and behavior of buyers. This flow of information, together with information on production costs, is crucial in the decision-making process for the next clothing collections.

In the commercialization circuit originated in La Salada and Feira da Madrugada marketplaces, other entrepreneurs have emerged, in this case playing the role of middlemen who buy wholesale and resell to retailers in other provinces. In the case of Brazil, they are called "sacoleiras." This is a garment commercialization system that uses long-distance buses to facilitate the evasion of certain taxes, thus keeping the cost of garments low. Similarly, maintaining low prices and ensuring business sustainability have incentivized the proliferation of marketplaces dedicated to the retail sale of fashionable garments in both countries. These marketplaces, known as Saladitas (Little Saladas) or Feirinhas da Madrugada (Little Feiras da Madrugada), capitalize on the allure associated with the origin of these clothes.

Finally, this Element argues that the opportunity structure encountered by entrepreneurs is shaped by institutional forces. Here, national and subnational governments and states in both countries play a key role. In addition to a variety of government responses to formalization of the labor force and informal enterprises, we argue that a key feature of the government response is regulatory forbearance. This Element documents that both entrepreneurs and actors involved in garment distribution do not comply with regulations because, in addition, governments adopt non-enforcement as an informal industrial policy aimed at allowing these economies to expand. Confronted with the dilemma of thriving, yet informal, garment circuits, governments tend to exercise forbearance rather than strictly enforce the numerous regulations being violated. This political economy perspective is important because it connects the web of institutional forces and interests with the structure and practice of meso-level agents, and micro-level entrepreneurs.

What do these circuits of low-cost fashion teach us? In the remainder of this introduction, we present some insights into the particularities of these economies vis-à-vis the common understanding of the garment industry, portrayed as part of global value chains and by far the most studied. The relevance of the cases studied in this Element lies in the fact that they reveal specific social features such as the assertion of the right to garment consumption by consumers excluded from formal stores; a generalization of informal processes that encompass the production, commercialization and consumption stages; and governments that, beyond attempts at formalization, adopt forbearance as a strategy for dealing with a phenomenon that exhibits structural features that are politically difficult to transform in the short term. In the following, we elaborate on three lessons at different levels learned from the cases analyzed in this Element.

At the micro level, the informal entrepreneurs and the business they develop must be seen as fundamental pillars on which this economy is sustained. If the business is to produce modinha, or a low-cost, aesthetically local form of fast-fashion, then monitoring consumer preferences becomes an imperative, which informs decisions about what the next products and cost structure will be. It goes without saying that creativity, based on one's own interpretation of customer desires and possibilities, plays a fundamental role in this process. Toward the end of this Element, we argue that this is a feature that distinguishes the circuits of La Salada and Feira da Madrugada from the classical model of global value chains.

Intermediaries who bridge producer networks and connect them with end consumers like the sacoleiras in Brazil are equally important. As Jiyhe Kim (2021) points out for the Argentine case, it is not just production units that reduce costs through non-compliance, but a strategy that extends to the entire distribution chain. The fact that informality extends to the end consumer shows us that we are witnessing a crucial difference between the distribution of garments according to the model of global value chains and that which takes place through formal channels.

At the macro level, the economies of La Salada and Feira da Madrugada point to the need to consider forbearance as a governmental strategy, both for electoral purposes (Holland 2017) and to create social order (Dewey 2020a, 2022). Of course, forbearance is not the only strategy employed by governments; they have also adopted other approaches such as formalization and repression. However, forbearance remains a significant and explanatory factor in the widespread informality previously mentioned. This is especially true because formalization efforts continuously exclude actors in these marketplaces, who then revert to informal practices. Forbearance emerges not only as a strategy to deal with a structural problem, but also as an informal strategy to boost the economy, a kind of informal industrial policy (Dewey and Di Carlo 2022). Also at the macro level, the cases analyzed show us that certain global trends, such as international value chains and the set of subprocesses involved (outsourcing, international division of labor, dominance of multinationals and large retailers, etc.), have certain limits. For those interested in analyzing how the garment industry is configured in different geographies, the case studies show that the explanatory power of the GVC paradigm is also limited.

Between producers, distributors, and vendors on one side, and planning and law enforcement agencies on the other, there are informal brokers and organizations operating at the meso level. Local associations and "managers," as they are known in La Salada, are involved in organizing these marketplaces entirely or partially, the distribution of clothes, and their regional satellite markets. They facilitate payments for leniency and protection from police officers, inspectors, and support for friendly politicians. They strive to maintain amicable relations with government officials and politicians who hold local power, securing protection from them in exchange for electoral support and political stability. Such politicians engage in these relationships and defend these circuits' activities because they recognize their economic importance and the costs associated with their disruption due to legal enforcement. These intermediaries make forbearance possible through systems of informal taxation or extortion, providing protection to producers and vendors while benefiting the involved politicians. Although socially legitimate, these intermediaries are informal in that they do not comply with various legal obligations. They are more influential and dominate the sheds in La Salada, each controlled by a manager, whereas in Feira da Madrugada, their activities are confined to the streets.

This Element is divided into six sections. The first section briefly explains the case selection criteria, describes the methodological strategy, and presents hypotheses that guide our analysis. After showing how demand for low-cost clothes contributes to the development of these circuits, the next section analyzes the supply side, that is, the entrepreneurs and the business model they have developed. We explain in this section in which sense we speak about informality in relation to the production, trade, and distribution in these circuits. The fifth section discusses how politicians and government officials have responded to the emergence and growth of La Salada and Feira da Madrugada and provides empirical evidence on forbearance as a government strategy. Finally, the last section reflects on the implications of both cases for our understanding of garment production and trade in Latin America (as emerging market economies) in relation to the extant literature and, notably, the role of global value chains and informality.

2 Research Design and Variables

This Element is the result of an exploratory joint analysis that combines and puts into dialogue extensive fieldwork and interviews in the circuits extending from La Salada and Feira da Madrugada, conducted by each of us: Matías Dewey studied La Salada, while André Vereta-Nahoum focused on Feira da Madrugada. All interviews in La Salada were conducted by Dewey, and those in Feira da Madrugada by Vereta-Nahoum. While we highlight the specificities of each circuit, we emphasize their many similarities to demonstrate how these circuits expand existing knowledge about the contemporary garment industry by challenging widely discussed trends.

As an exploratory analysis of two marketplaces and their circuits in Argentina and Brazil, this Element uses deviant case analysis to examine a case that well-established theories cannot predict. Both cases are judged deviant "relative to some general model of causal relations" (Gerring 2006, 106). The commodity-chain approach to economic development predicts that poor working conditions in sweatshops are closely associated with garment companies' relocation of labor-intensive manufacturing operations to developing countries. In this picture, the production stage tends to feature relatively higher levels of informality, while the commercialization of finished garments runs mostly following legal norms. Therefore, the commodity-chain approach to economic development cannot explain extended forms of garment provision – as in countries such as Argentina and Brazil –

characterized by a myriad of informal marketplaces specialized in the commercialization of sweatshop-produced garments. The theory can also not predict the presence of workshops located downstream, that is, close to the consumer and without any connection with well-established brands. Notably, the contention about the emergence of a new garment production and distribution form in Argentina and Brazil does not mean the absence of garment companies integrated into GVC. We argue that both forms of production and distribution coexist.

Thus, this Element aims to test alternative explanations for these regional low-cost fashion circuits. Firstly, we postulate that sudden economic booms and busts played a crucial role in the emergence and resilience of these circuits. While the garment sector continues to be an important employment-generating industry, deindustrialization and productive restructuring processes in both countries have led to a reduction in employment within this sector. As a result, creative and skilled labor forces have become available for the workshops. Former employees' know-how and facilities became crucial factors for the emergence of workshops managed by former garment employees. Low-cost fashion circuits would provide opportunities with low entry barriers, explaining the supply.

Furthermore, rapidly changing national economic conditions witnessed in the first decade of the 2000s produced higher consumption aspirations and higher social status on lower- and middle-income social strata, followed by crises with dramatic effects on their purchasing power. This would create an ongoing, yet variable, demand for fashionable low-cost clothes with unique symbolic local features that mirror the different economic outlooks of Argentina and Brazil.

Secondly, these two circuits have significantly benefited from the influx of migrants, mainly from Korea, Bolivia, and China, who have established businesses in the garment sector and supply labor. During the 1990s, wage differentials and well-rooted ethnic and kinship networks acted as pull factors attracting large numbers of migrants to La Salada and Feira da Madrugada. These migrants became integrated into an already highly informal industry and are now vital actors in producing and distributing low-cost fashion. As such, they could contribute to the supply of low-cost fashion.

Thirdly, the role of government agencies and politicians is equally important in understanding the development and competitiveness of these circuits. The realization that production, trade, and distribution involve significant degrees of informality in both circuits not only serves as a hypothesis to justify the price competitiveness of their clothes but also highlights the importance of understanding state attitudes, particularly leniency. Sudden economic transformations are a necessary, but insufficient, condition to explain their emergence and development. We argue that these transformations are buffered and processed by the respective governments through the manipulation of various enforcement mechanisms. We hypothesize that forbearance has been an important strategy for responding to production and trade that are difficult to manage yet essential to the local economies.

The productive structures of both countries (characterized by widespread and deeply entrenched sectorial informality, varying access to garments among the population, uncontrolled migration flows, etc.) make regulatory forbearance a more effective approach than alternative lawful industrial policies (Dewey and Di Carlo 2022), particularly in promoting the garment industry. Governments' strategic use of forbearance is sometimes coupled with policies aimed at the formalization of street vendors and the promotion of petty entrepreneurship. Different responses by local and federal officials, as well as the role of politicians as possible intermediaries, are also explored.

In the following sections we analyze each of these variables (booms and busts, migration, the creativity of producers, and informality) and how they relate to the demand, supply, and the differing roles that state agents and politicians play (forbearance, repression, and formalization).

3 The Demand for Low-Cost Fashion: Consumers, Marketplaces, and Inland Distribution

Every Tuesday and Friday evening, Ana dons her pink uniform, bids farewell to her children, and boards her van. By midnight, she will have already picked up all her clients from their homes in São José dos Campos and will join other vans and buses from her company on the Governor Carvalho Pinto Highway, bound for Brás in downtown São Paulo. With some luck, the caravan arrives at the parking lot of All Brás – a large shopping center – by 2 a.m., just as the main streets of the neighborhood are already bustling with thousands of small stalls adorned with dangling lights, offering affordable clothing items. Alongside the stalls, the popular malls and galleries begin to open, and the spacious warehouse where the Feira da Madrugada operates comes to life.

Delays can be cruel: most excursions, like Ana's, return to their cities of origin on the same day, in the early or mid-afternoon when the shops and malls in Brás close, and the stalls have long cleared the streets for traffic. Ana's vans and buses never leave after two o'clock in the afternoon. Her clients, like the majority of travelers who arrive in Brás on these buses and vans, therefore have less than twelve hours to do their shopping. They come to Brás in the early morning, often "in pursuit of fashion," as Maria de Fátima, one of Ana's clients, says, to acquire merchandise – clothes and accessories – that they resell in their cities of origin.

Maria de Fátima is a client of Ana's tours to Feira da Madrugada, and she has been coming to Brás at least monthly for the last thirty years. Initially, she came to complement her income as a seamstress in a local industry by delivering parcels of clothes ordered by a friend and shop owner. Over the last decade, she has transitioned into being a "sacoleira" or bag carrier in Portuguese, buying pieces she mostly sells to her former colleagues in front of the firm where she used to work. She notes that tastes have changed, and there is now a demand for simpler, cheaper clothes. Low-cost fashion refers to this type of fashion that Maria alludes to that retains fashion symbols but is affordable to lower- and middle-income groups in Brazil and Argentina, who are often excluded from traditional garment retail shops.

Shop owners, street vendors, and intermediaries are some of the key players in an important circuit of clothing trade that has Brás as its distribution hub. Drivers, guides, and loaders complete the population of this circuit and move millions of reais daily throughout the country, along with people and merchandise.

This scene is multiplied by thousands in both Feira da Madrugada and La Salada. Every night, thousands of buses and vans park in lots across Brás and Ingeniero Budge, bringing dozens of thousands of buyers. La Salada and Feira da Madrugada are marketplaces that serve as nodes that connect the local production of inexpensive clothes with distribution networks that spread over not only Brazil and Argentina but also neighboring countries. They are wholesale markets catering to a large extent to thousands of daily buyers who resell garments in their hometowns. Beyond the streets, roads, and commercial spaces of Feira da Madrugada and La Salada, this circuit generates important digital flows. Communication channels, particularly mobile phones and the worldwide web, play a crucial role in promoting this circuit by disseminating information, images, and messages that connect buyers, transporters, and sellers located in different places. These circuits thrive on the ability of these channels to enhance the appeal of the region and its clothing. However, the distribution circuit of popular fashion depends on the mobile agency of a group of women who facilitate trade between Brás and La Salada and millions of consumers in various cities across Brazil, Argentina, and neighboring countries. As they distribute clothing merchandise from La Salada and Feira da Madrugada, they also act as important intermediaries of the symbols that give them value and meaning. In other words, they help shaping and simultaneously take advantage of a form of low-cost, popular fashion (Vereta-Nahoum 2021). In Figure 1, we see a group of buyers taking their purchases to the buses that will take them back to their hometowns where they resell clothes bought at La Salada.

Figure 1 A group of buyers take their purchases to the buses that will take them back to their hometowns where they resell clothes bought at La Salada

Although this group is considerably heterogeneous, this activity is predominantly carried out by women. Despite advances in communication means, cost reduction, and increased speed in transportation, many still come to Feira da Madrugada and La Salada to discover trends, acquire novelties, and strengthen relationships maintained with suppliers in the region. They often say they need to touch the fabric to assess the quality of the clothes and do not trust online retailers. The limits of digital commerce for these traders lie in the challenge of evaluating garment quality and monitoring trends they disseminate across the countries. Lower prices often mean lower-quality fabrics and techniques, but these traders still seek the best affordable and trendy clothes in an attempt to shape and meet consumer tastes and purchasing power.

Some of these resellers have stalls in the streets and marketplaces in their towns, known as "feiras da madrugada" in Brazil and "saladitas" in Argentina, using the name of the place of origin of the clothes as a brand and organizational model for their commercial activities. Even though the reality of these markets is very volatile and difficult to measure, a survey by the Argentine Confederation of Medium Enterprises (CAME) in May 2017 listed 662 informal markets in 110 locations, totaling more than 63,000 stalls (Infobae 2017). These street and built marketplaces function as regional distribution centers, providing wholesale opportunities for smaller resellers and retail options for final consumers. They not only lure consumers by offering much-praised goods from the largest cities in

Argentina and Brazil but also replicate on a smaller scale the vibrant atmosphere found in La Salada and Feira da Madrugada.

While purchasing goods from regional "saladitas" and "feirinhas" for door-to-door sales or known clients is an accessible option for low-income traders, buying wholesale in São Paulo and Buenos Aires is not feasible. The activity of national distribution of clothes requires a significant amount of floating capital for travel and the purchase of clothes. Nor is it necessarily carried out by informal traders. They form, in fact, a heterogeneous group with a variety of arrangements and business models, from street sellers and "sacoleiras," as traveling saleswomen are called in Brazil, owners of medium and large stores in cities in the interior of the country, as well as resellers who travel by plane and owners of retail chains in medium-sized towns who visit the areas to become acquainted with new trends and replenish their stock. The case of Maria de Fátima mentioned previously indicates that many women involved in this business had previous professional involvement with clothes, such as being producers, store salespersons, intermediaries for other resellers, or even fashion designers. This practical "tricks of the trade" knowledge seems essential for success in the business and explains their role in creating a specific form of fashion that operates within a circuit influenced by, but independent from, global clothing retailers.

Eventually, they purchase clothes in other production centers, but often assert that Feira da Madrugada and La Salada have more diversity. These stores follow different business models, including wholesalers that act as regional distributors, stores with fixed prices, and retailers. While street sellers and traveling saleswomen normally focus on a specific type of clothes (athletic, children's, basic pieces, religious-oriented, and plus-sized are just a few of the niches they pursue) and work with loyal clients, catering to their particular taste (see Vereta-Nahoum 2021), shop owners complement their offer with other merchandise such as accessories, handbags, perfumes, and toys. Some successful retailers that began selling clothes as traveling saleswomen and have prevailed over the years opening shops share tales of socioeconomic mobility. While the majority sell clothes for the lower classes, some reported having customers from wealthier classes in their smaller cities.

The circuits formed by these marketplaces and the multiple sales points maintained by resellers throughout Argentina and Brazil reproduce some specific characteristics of fast fashion, but with lower prices than those practiced by global brands. The models have a very fast turnover, a feature highlighted by the resellers, and they conform to their own trends, with an aesthetic that is appreciated throughout the countries. These models are not based directly on prêt-à-porter fashion but on pieces observed in television shows, especially soap operas, music videos, and digital platforms such as YouTube and Instagram.

They adapt these trends and models to form what is natively called in Brazil "modinha," which, in turn, influences trends in the rest of the country. Modinha is a widespread native concept, a common term traders use to categorize the clothes they sell, to name their shops, or to advertise products on the internet. La Salada equally trades garments that reflect fashion trends that are envisaged and produced locally.

Many of these resellers, like Maria de Fátima, state this clearly: they travel in search of "modinha." It refers to basic clothes with significant demand for quick turnover (less than a month, they say), seasonal, and particularly associated with celebrities. Despite its diminutive form, which semantically indicates its cost, the production and dissemination of "modinha" follow the fashion logic described by Blumer (1969): it begins with an organized movement in the sector that translates tastes into models, followed by games of imitation and distinction that select which of these models will become prevalent. In the case of "modinha," local producers adapt celebrity images to create models that are then tested with resellers and, through them, with their consumers. The designs are created and produced in workshops that monitor fashion trends on TV and the internet. Christian, who has worked as a salesperson and producer in Feira da Madrugada, explains the process:

> Do you remember that soap opera with Jeiza, played by Paola Oliveira last year? I used to bring a ribbed knit dress [that she wore on set], and it sold like crazy [...]. If it's on the soap opera, if someone famous is wearing it ... you know how it is, right? People want to be the same, so whoever brought it in, sold a lot, like 1000 pieces per day. Sometimes even up to 5000 pieces per day.

"Modinha" is also fueled by virtual promoters of popular fashion on Instagram, Facebook, YouTube, and TikTok who display these pieces and indicate where to buy them. Numerous videos titled "latest modinha" or "unmissable clothes in Feira da Madrugada" showcase the same images that buyers consume and must be familiar to resellers. These shared cultural forms that flow through digital platforms and electronic communication help coordinate production, distribution, and consumption, reducing uncertainty (Kawamura 2005). Without using the term "modinha," Maria has been selling "fashionable" clothes purchased in the market of La Salada for twenty years. Her customers are other wholesalers who resell in other places in Córdoba, and retailers who resell in their neighborhoods. On several occasions, Maria has paid for advertising on Facebook and shares her website in other groups on the same network specialized in garments from La Salada, in addition to using WhatsApp as a contact agenda and to disseminate products through mailing lists.

There is a group of women who dedicate themselves to promoting Brás fashion in the virtual realm, using YouTube and Instagram accounts. Resellers often arrive at the markets with images on their phones of what they are looking for. Producers commit to producing them in the agreed quantity within a short period of time. Therefore, it is ultimately the resellers who determine the success of the models tested by producers every week, and producers understand they must cater to their demand. By blending these images with knowledge of the taste preferences of end consumers, they select what defines "modinha" and set trends for the producers. They are, together with the producers and digital intermediaries, true fashionistas. They translate their knowledge of the cultural and aesthetic forms of low-income families into this specific form of fashion (Haddad and Castro 2019), which can hardly be replicated elsewhere without the monitoring practices bridged with the direct contact resellers have with consumers.

The allure of fashion is a prominent factor that explains the number of individuals working in these distribution circuits. Among them, numerous women have received formal training in fashion design and exhibit a genuine passion for the industry. Engaging in the selection and distribution of garments allows them to express this interest, especially in labor markets where opportunities for fashion designers are limited. In the Brazilian context, the expansion of higher education during the twenty-first century resulted in a rise in the number of fashion designers. In 2019, fifty-two universities in Brazil offered bachelor degrees in fashion (FOLHA 2019). However, the labor market failed to absorb all the graduates.

"Modinha" adds value and competitiveness to garments produced in Feira da Madrugada and La Salada. While the clothing retail sector in Brazil relies on technological innovation and upgrading to face international competition (see e.g. Piore and Cardoso 2019), workers in low-cost garment districts in Sao Paulo and Buenos Aires add an intangible value – modinha – and resort to a business model that makes international competition more challenging. Despite occasional complaints about the decline in clothing quality, resellers often assert their preference for locally produced garments as long as the prices remain low.

Isabel, who has been in the business in Brazil for three decades, illustrates this attitude. She used to buy clothes at a different garment district in São Paulo, Bom Retiro, where purchases have better quality, but nowadays people want cheap clothes that she needs to sell if she wants to stay in business. She laments, "This makes me opt for simpler products." However, the goods produced there are still considered superior to Chinese imports, which she only buys when absolutely necessary: "I don't like working with clothes that come from abroad, except when I am forced to. (. . .) There is no proper mannequin, the quality, the fabric, it is not like the ones manufactured in Brazil." Maria de Fatima agrees: while she used to buy exclusively from stores in Brás, she now primarily purchases from stalls in shopping centers. The clothes found in the streets, particularly Chinese imports, are not suitable for her clientele. Selling them would damage her reputation. Despite the changes, Brás continues to offer the variety and prices that people want, making it the go-to place in Brazil.

Modinha is not only preferred on aesthetic and quality grounds but also demands a quick turnover, making sending designs, producing them, and importing them to Brazil more difficult. Geared toward generating frequent consumption, "modinha" pieces, as indicated by resellers, are very ephemeral and quickly replaced. If these items are not sold shortly after purchase, the chances of selling them decrease significantly. The Brazilian store owner Esmeralda recounts:

> You can't rely too much on 'modinha' because it changes every week. I bought an open jumpsuit that the girl from the 8 p.m. soap opera was wearing, I bought two, and one is already stuck because it's getting colder, no one will wear an open jumpsuit.

Consequently, imported clothes, especially those from Asian countries, can hardly compete in the "modinha" niche. It is no surprise that the imported garments sold in Feira da Madrugada and La Salada are typically brand-inspired athletic and very basic pieces, such as T-shirts, socks, and underwear. In sum, there is a combination of price, quality, and taste that explains the advantages of locally produced clothes over imported ones.

The persistence of inland distribution circuits is closely intertwined with long-term economic trends and state policies. Economic booms have driven a surge in national clothing consumption, and social policies that resulted in monetary expansion in Brazil and Argentina led to increased clothing expenses, particularly in smaller towns. These developments have created fresh opportunities for women willing to supply these regions with clothes. Additionally, the expansion of university education in fashion design has contributed to the growth of this workforce and the supply we analyze in the next section. Conversely, economic crises and the restructuring of production in both countries have resulted in a decline in formal employment, prompting many women to turn to clothing distribution as their primary occupation or as a supplementary source of income (Vereta-Nahoum 2021).

The distribution of garments from Feira da Madrugada and La Salada is closely connected to initiatives promoting popular consumption of clothes, entrepreneurship, and formalization, particularly through monotributo and

MEI schemes. These policies have been more advantageous for traders than for clothing producers. Furthermore, forbearance through the selective enforcement of taxation plays a residual role in the distribution of clothes, as some women transport goods by buses to circumvent inter-state taxes. However, it is crucial to note that incorporated businesses, MEIs, and monotributistas do pay taxes on final sales, ensuring compliance with tax regulations.

Marketplaces

The circuits of production and distribution of low-cost fashion in Brazil and Argentina find their primary trade nodes in La Salada and Feira da Madrugada. They are marketplaces in the most fundamental sense of places where thousands of persons meet to exchange multiple goods, some of which are auxiliary to the trade of low-cost garments. Their attractiveness made the space in the streets, sheds, galleries, and shopping centers a much disputed and profitable asset. Their emergence and daily operation are grounded on a material infrastructure that distributes and organizes producers, traders, and spaces for consumers. This infrastructure is the result of the initiatives of traders and partly the action of political actors over the past decades. As confluence for sellers and buyers of low-cost garments, they have been areas of continuous interventions by local governments, politicians, and party delegates with different moods, intentions, and conceptions of the place and its trade activities, from repression to legitimation and active promotion. These interventions reflect views not only of informal economic activities but also of urban retail spaces.

Our goal in this section is to retrace the formation and development of these marketplaces and identify commonalities and differences that explain their emergence, location, and particular dynamics. In the last section of this section, we will discuss the politics of space surrounding La Salada and Feira da Madrugada, indicating how urban planners and other political actors compete to organize these places. These places in Argentina and Brazil, where producers and consumers meet over low-cost fashion – an economic good and a cultural form – rely on specific material and socioeconomic conditions and political construction that reflect political attitudes. The last section in this Element will better explore the changing political attitudes toward the production and trade of low-cost fashion in various forms of formality. However, here we discuss the reflection of these attitudes, narratives, and policies in the spatial organization of these two marketplaces and the legitimation of their traders. In doing so, we want to highlight the importance of their material infrastructure. Studies in the sociology of finances have focused on the materiality of financial markets, their relationship to the performance of expert theories of market exchange, and disputes surrounding their organization (Mackenzie 2009; Pardo-Guerra 2019; Zaloom 2006). Garcia-Parpet's (1986) study of an auction market for strawberries pioneered this line of research and extended its findings to markets for agricultural produce. Cochoy (2007) explored how objects organize the interactions in supermarkets. And despite the lack of studies on the material organization of seemingly informal markets, there is no reason why such marketplaces should be less reliant on material infrastructures, their organization, and objects less controversial or unimportant to the interactions.

La Salada and Feira da Madrugada: Conditions behind Their Emergence

La Salada and Feira da Madrugada are relatively new marketplaces that emerged in an age of increasing globalization. Their expansion and success strongly rely on the specific conditions that were locally available and the allure they generate among consumers. These are the places where the demand for and supply of low-cost fashion converge, making it essential to explain their constitution and development.

They are in very different locations in the urbanscape of the two largest metropolises in South America. While La Salada is located in a previous balneary resort that served in the mid-twentieth century as a weekend playground for the industrial working class in Lomas de Zamora, some 20 kilometers (12 miles) from Central Buenos Aires, Feira da Madrugada is located in Brás, a central district in Sao Paulo known for a century as a textile and then garment district.

Despite these differences, these marketplaces' creation and development processes share strong similarities. Beginning in the 1990s, their development was strongly influenced by specific patterns of the Argentine and Brazilian national economies – booms and crises – and policies that championed the expansion of consumption to the least wealthy and the recognition of the importance of informal trade to the national economies. They also benefited from similar and pendular influxes of migrant producers from Andean countries that sought to capitalize on the fluctuation of currency exchange rates of the Peso in Argentina and the Real in Brazil.

Traders built them among ruins of the industrial era in areas that offered the necessary resources for them to thrive. They had already tried their luck in other commercial districts but looked for a place and a time to place their stalls and trade their goods unencumbered. In both cases, this meant initially establishing night markets, and thus both marketplaces became famous because of their trading activities in the small hours. In La Salada and Feira da Madrugada, these spaces offered a unique opportunity for producers to sell directly to consumers and eliminate intermediaries. They discovered that they could generate higher profits in Buenos Aires and São Paulo by selling low-cost wholesale clothing locally rather than working for brands and stores that outsourced their production to their workshops.

The evidence suggests that La Salada commenced its operations as a center for distributing garments in the mid-1990s. Before that time, La Salada served as a health resort and recreational facility owned by labor unions, providing an opportunity for individuals to access experiences previously exclusive to those who had leisure time. This included the chance to visit facilities featuring thermal salty waters. The growth and decline of La Salada as a recreational center aligned with the rise and fall of a society built on labor and safeguarded by both unions and governmental institutions.

By the early 1990s, circumstances led to the establishment of an informal garment economy with an internal dynamic different from the formal sector. These included a significant population of unemployed individuals, many of whom had prior experience in the garment industry and were willing to produce garments from their homes. Additionally, the suburban region faced economic and infrastructural challenges, while a considerable portion of society, facing increasing impoverishment, was in dire need of essential garment items but faced growing barriers to access. These factors collectively paved the path for the development of La Salada, transitioning it from a place centered around mineral-water pools to a bustling garment marketplace.

If La Salada found an idle infrastructure to grow, Feira da Madrugada always had to compete with well-established trade in busy commercial areas. Self-organized street vendors of clothes established the first instance of what became known as Feira da Madrugada (roughly Dawn Market, in English translation) in the early 2000s at a bustling shopping street known for low-cost goods of all sorts in the historical center of São Paulo, March 25th Street. Street vendors already took the street during commercial hours, and thus the new vendors placed their stalls in the street and sidewalks during the late night and early morning (thus its name).

This did not prevent them from entering into bitter conflicts with other street vendors and shop owners at the adjacent Municipal market for fresh produce that also operated at night. With the assistance of police forces, the local government evicted the garment traders who found a new area less than a kilometer east in the Brás neighborhood. In 2003, newspapers began to report on the new "Dawn Market" that took place in the night and early morning in the central square and adjacent streets of Brás, with the initial tolerance of the local district government (Folha 2003a).

Brás had been a vital garment district for the twentieth century, producing and selling wholesale fabrics and clothes. Over the decades, Italians, Levantine, Brazilian Northeastern, and Andean migrants created and populated small factories, workshops, and stores (Andrade 1991). Brás became the main area for buying wholesale low-cost clothing in the country. It retains this place in the public imagination as the best place to find bargains in jeans, trendy outfits, fitness apparel, socks, underwear, and inexpensive garments in general. Consequently, thousands of shoppers from Brazil, the neighboring countries, and even Angola visit *Feira da Madrugada* to buy garments, mostly to resell in their hometowns. Many shopping bus tours to Brás arrived at night and used a derelict depot from the national railroad company to park.

Due to this tradition, it only seemed logical for vendors to establish the Dawn Market in the area. But even more, similar to what happened in La Salada, many of the soon-to-be vendors of Feira da Madrugada were already in the area, working in the workshops to produce clothes. They realized they could sell their production directly to thousands of consumers instead of producing for brands and shops, and thus increase their revenues. But local politicians soon began to call for law enforcement against unlawful use of street space. Facing repression or extortion from the police in the streets, many vendors looked at the abandoned depot and other industrial buildings and warehouses in the area as a good alternative. In an interview with a national newspaper, the informal "manager" who controlled the parking lot at the depot recalls that "Street vendors started to ask to stay in the area. Since buses arrived early, [people] bought from them. The Popular Dawn Shopping was inaugurated in August 2005" (Magalhães 2011). This also seemed an excellent solution to the Municipal government seeking to empty the streets from traders without further consideration for the public nature of the depot – owned by the Federal state, which controlled the railroad company (Folha 2003b).

At first, stalls were negotiated by a private firm and associations formed by traders, which also organized the space, its activities, and services, regulating qualified agents and forms of trade, often with conflicts over the ability to negotiate stalls. These meso-level agents were very important initially, with many self-named "traders associations" negotiating stall space and protection from police and inspectors. At the depot, a manager mediated an extortion scheme with Federal authorities (Magalhães 2011).

The local government, gaining the right to use the depot from the Federal government in 2010, vowed to create new facilities, comply with counterfeit laws and safety regulations, and legally distribute stalls. They built a vast, single-story marketplace, later demolished in 2018 when the space was given to a private firm under a state-planned concession to build a proper shopping center. In addition to the building of a multistory shopping mall that retains its "popular," that is, low-cost nature, the winner of the concession had to commit to a series of infrastructural improvements defined in a plan that the project division of the National Economic and Social Development Bank of Brazil (BNDES) developed. This would eventually result in the current New "Dawn Market Shopping Center" after a bitter conflict that involved Judicial challenges to the concession by representatives of associations of traders and a Special Hearing Commission at the Town Hall.

These are some of the conditions that explain the continuing supply of low-cost clothes in these marketplaces. However, they would not persist without a continuing local presence of consumers demanding the goods traded in these spaces. The ongoing demand explaining these thriving marketplaces is no less socioeconomically and culturally constructed than the supply. Competition from other producing areas and online retail could have erased this marketplace. This was not the case, however, due to the constant flow of consumers interested in buying, mainly wholesale, specific fashion models produced in those regions. Partly because they look for images that circulate nationally, associated with what they name, in Brazil, "modinha."

In the case of Feira da Madrugada, located in Brás, wholesale consumers were already there looking for clothes they could resell in their cities. They already knew that the area presented them with good bargaining opportunities: they could find low-cost clothes catering to their consumers' tastes. The Dawn Market only increased the influx of consumers to Brás. Many interviewees asserted that Brazil's marketplace has no rival for its diverse offer and reasonable prices. Hundreds of buses arrive daily from other states, in some cases after long journeys, crowded with wholesale buyers who resell clothes at their or at their clients' homes, stores, or even at smaller dawn markets in other cities. This is, just like La Salada, mostly a wholesale marketplace.

The strong association of these urban areas with low-cost garments in the minds of many and the offer of specific fashion designs inspired by celebrities and rapidly tested with consumers are complemented by broader socioeconomic shifts and policies toward consumption. To comprehend the demand that drives these circuits, it is imperative to consider the exceptional surge in demand for low-cost garments in the past decades. This market dynamic is closely tied to a more extensive socio-structural transformation that extends beyond the boundaries of this particular industry and points to the problem of accessing clothing. Many cannot afford garment items in authorized stores, shopping malls, and other legally established shops. From this standpoint, these marketplaces and the workshop-based economy it embodies can be seen as adaptive responses to the prevailing macro-level social arrangement.

In the next section, we present the specific socioeconomic conditions in Brazil and Argentina that explain the national economic differences that nonetheless similarly promoted the growth of the circuits centered in Feira da Madrugada and La Salada.

Sudden Economic Booms and Busts

Sudden economic transformations and the outlook of the formal economies in Argentina and Brazil have been, and continue to be, crucial to developing the circuits around La Salada and Feira da Madrugada. Notably, both circuits have emerged in the context of preexisting garment industries, meaning that they developed experiencing continuous transfers of labor, know-how of different types, networks of contacts, or capital. However, these linkages emerged and intensified due to sudden changes in which the low-cost garment sector acts as recipients of labor, capital, and know-how.

The low-cost fashion circuits that developed around La Salada and Feira da Madrugada provided two positive externalities to cushion sudden economic booms and bursts: income for producers and vendors, since the garment-manufacturing and reselling businesses do not have very high entry barriers, and cheap garments for new low-income consumers or those experiencing declining incomes. Next we describe some of these changes in both countries and some national differences.

While La Salada thrived initially as a countercyclical response to crises and declining purchasing power, growing further during the recovery period in the 2000s, Feira da Madrugada emerged during a period of economic growth, catering to an expanding market for clothes. Later, during the recession of 2015–2017, it offered a lower-cost alternative to more expensive options from larger retailers and provided income opportunities for the unemployed.

In the case of the low-cost fashion circuit in Argentina, the progressive general economic deterioration and instability are reflected in the emergence of the marketplace and the surrounding production units. Once a place of recreation with saltwater pools for the working class, the "Balneario y Parque La Salada" began to decline in the early 1960s due to saltwater contamination. Its closure marked the start of the area's socioeconomic decline. Many current La Salada marketplace workers were affected by the closure or relocation of businesses in the 1960s (Rougier and Pampin 2015, 209). This decline became more severe from the mid-1970s onward with the military government's economic policies.

However, the general situation in the metropolitan area was no better. Between the military coup that ousted Isabel Peron in 1976 and the early 1990s, workers throughout the region experienced massive job destruction. According to Vio and

Cabrera (2015, 257), this socioeconomic decline extended beyond the poor segments of society to include the middle sectors, which began facing serious employment and income problems in a hyperinflationary context. In the mid-1990s, when the garment economy began to emerge around the La Salada marketplace, the unemployment rate in the Buenos Aires Metropolitan Area (the conurbano) was as high as 22 percent.

Workers' testimonies help explain the connection between the depressed national economy and the emergence of a low-cost fashion circuit centered on La Salada. Most agree that La Salada's activities peaked in 2001 when the formal economy experienced its worst crisis. Garment entrepreneurs, workers, vendors, seamstresses, wholesalers, transporters, fabric and accessories sellers recognize that those years were the peak of this circuit that offered income opportunities – in a sector focused on a staple good such as clothing – to those whose opportunities in the formal sector had diminished.

As Gustavo Ludmer (2020) explains, the macroeconomic change that contributed decisively to the productive and commercial success of the La Salada marketplace was the end of the so-called peso-dollar convertibility. While a significant portion of the products sold in the La Salada marketplace in the 1990s were imported garments, the devaluation of the currency in 2002 led to substituting these imports with garments produced in informal workshops near the marketplace.

The economic development in the following years strengthened growth across all sectors – production, distribution, and consumption – allowing La Salada to establish itself as the leading supplier of essential clothing and low-cost fashion. The economic recovery that began in 2002 was marked by the expansion and growth of this circuit, including the multiplication of production units, an increase in informal employment, and a sharp rise in clothing consumption (Kosacoff et al. 2004, 19; Tavosnanska 2010, 72). Additionally, the protectionist measures introduced from that year on benefited not only the formal garment industry but also stimulated the growth of the informal sector. Consequently, the growth of the formal economy did not necessarily lead to a transfer of labor from the informal sector to the formal one.

Feira da Madrugada is equally tied to the decline of industrial activities and its socioeconomic effects, especially in urban unemployment and abandonment of vast industrial spaces. In this case, it is situated in what was once an industrial district in central São Paulo. The economic liberalization and appreciation of the Brazilian Real during the 1990s significantly affected the national textile industry. Until the 1990s, Brazil established a robust protectionist approach to development, and the textile and garment industries were no exception (Abreu 2004; Hiratuka and Garcia, 1995; Monteiro Filha and Correa 2002). Following trade liberalization, the sector underwent restructuring in order to enhance competitiveness.

Analyses indicate that imports affected the textile industry more than the garment industry. Imports of garments went down over the first half of the 1990s (Hiratuka and Garcia 1995, 15). This is often attributed to competitive advantages on labor and energy costs in the country (Hiratuka and Garcia 1995; Monteiro Filha and Correa 2002). These advantages are, in turn, linked to the widespread availability of skilled and relatively inexpensive labor in workshops, primarily in Brás and increasingly in other areas of Sao Paulo. Although not entirely new to the sector, outsourcing production to workshops became more prevalent as part of the strategies employed by several firms, fostering activities in the area. The industry has retained its status as one of the largest in the world, primarily due to the sizable national market and significant clothing consumption within the country.

However, while La Salada emerged amid a bitter economic crisis, Feira da Madrugada thrived during the economic recovery, taking advantage of the existing production infrastructure. When the demand for inexpensive garments burgeoned, and the number of daily buyers increased, the skilled workers in workshops began to sell their production, individually or in networks cemented by kinship and common origin ties. The growth of formal employment and a global higher sensibility toward corporate social responsibility highlighted the use of abusive working practices by big garment retail groups. Increased oversight by labor inspectors and attorneys and exemplary court cases against the most prominent groups also pushed them away from workshops.

Over the first decade of the twenty-first century, economic growth led to the expansion of formal employment and a significant poverty reduction. There is a scholarly disagreement about the extent of this reduction and its effects in terms of social mobility and inequality (for a good overview, see Souza 2010; Neri 2011; Ferreira et al. 2013; Scalon and Salata 2012; Kerstenetzky, Uchôa, and Silva 2015). The actual socioeconomic meaning of the category coined to identify the families that emerged from poverty – "the new middle class" – admittedly with a prospective sense (Neri 2011) was also debated. For our purposes, what is more important is to notice that as an administrative category created by the government (Kopper & Damo 2018), it suggests a political project to increase access to consumption goods that express class status (Yaccoub 2011). The project included access to higher education and formal employment as well, but the expression of belonging to a new middle class, just like to the middle classes before (O'Dougherty 1998), was equally associated with the status bestowed upon consumption, even with a real income that was not significantly different from the income they had before. The so-called "new middle class" might not differ substantially in their income, consumption patterns, dwellings, and access to essential services from the lower strata of society (Kerstenetzky, Uchôa, and Silva 2015). However, family budget surveys show increased access to consumption goods in Brazilian households, notably in poorer areas of the country. More importantly, this mobility out of poverty increased the number of potential clothing consumers. These families appropriated the category and were eager to consume more and express the new perceived status of the "new middle class" through garments. With limited income to spend, they looked for reasonable prices in models that reflected their tastes. Producers, shop owners, and traveling salespersons across the country realized this opportunity, and Feira da Madrugada offered this sort of good that they recognized as precisely what their consumers were looking for: modinha. Many of the shop owners interviewed assert that this popular, low-cost variation of fast fashion, with equally quick turnaround, is what they can sell.

When economic growth and the political project involving the social mobility of low-income families ended in Brazil in 2015, the crisis also promoted demand for low-cost clothes, especially among impoverished middle classes trying to keep their status and provide clothing to their families. Brás offered producers interested in better deals for their work, a daily influx of consumers of wholesale garments, and disputed spaces.

Demand and Infrastructures

Having presented the conditions behind the emergence and development of La Salada and Feira da Madrugada, we now depict their internal organization. Some features already existed during their creation: large physical spaces that gather thousands of stalls distributed over long rows in spatially organized spaces that differ in both cases. The low prices of the clothes they sell result from high sales volume, a shorter distribution chain because most vendors are also involved in producing the garments they sell, and sheer tax evasion. They are producer-vendors. This means that they sell goods they produce directly, without intermediaries. The volume of sales and business opportunities in this space are directly linked to the daily influx of thousands of wholesale consumers. La Salada and Feira da Madrugada are busy spaces that attract tens of thousands of consumers per day and more during holidays; they are primarily wholesale marketplaces catering to consumers who frequently come from different cities and even countries to buy clothes they later resell. La Salada and Feira da Madrugada offer other types of products; most of its merchandise consists of low-cost garments. In this sense, they are the main distribution centers for low-cost garments in South America. The significant demand for affordable clothing aligns with the interests of garment manufacturers. In fact, given the minimal profit margins per single item and the presence of flexible labor, producers are primarily focused on the wholesale sector rather than retail. Moreover, the wholesale business facilitates heightened sales within a marketplace setting through increased interactions between buyers and sellers.

The relatively short time these consumers have to purchase their goods and return to their cities on buses makes these very hectic places where people and carts are always moving quickly. The elusive sociality this setting promotes allows for relative anonymity, bargaining, and haggling with traders and producers. They share many characteristics of Geertz's Sefrou Suq (Geertz 1979), notably the opacity of price and quality that demand from consumers particular skills and local knowledge. While some imported goods, mainly branded athletic outfits, can be found in these spaces, most of the garments sold are locally produced.

Their existence is particularly intriguing in an age of online retail that has not replaced them. Even throughout the Covid-19 pandemic, they did not shut down for extended periods. Hundreds of buses from various corners of Argentina and Brazil persisted in arriving daily.[1] Saleswomen who were interviewed at Feira da Madrugada frequently asserted that they prefer to travel long distances to assess the quality of pieces and to get information about what is fashionable, or "modinha." They sometimes make orders in advance but often travel to ensure they buy good saleable clothes (Vereta-Nahoum 2021).

The internet and new communication technologies do play a role in organizing demand. First, they share valuable information about opportunities that assist visitors and consumers. Forums and groups on social networking sites share this information about how to move around these vast marketplaces and tips for first-time visitors. A number of buyers also maintain specialized YouTube channels with videos that advertise specific shops and trendy models. Some gave up on reselling clothes and have turned to these videos as their primary source of income. This helps to distribute the basic skills and local knowledge required to successfully buy clothes to resell without eliminating the advantages of skillful and experienced buyers who dominate the tricks of the trade. Apart from monitoring, it is also helpful to manufacture modinha, that is, disseminate models ordered to those who buy goods in these places by their consumers. Second, the communication technologies that the internet

---

[1] La Salada was closed for around six months, that is, longer than Feira da Madrugada. Having the marketplace closed, informal garment producers were forced to rely heavily on digital tools such as digital payment services or closed Facebook communities and postal services to ship orders. However, as soon as the government lifted pandemic-related restrictions, buyers started again traveling to the marketplaces (Dewey 2022).

enables create new channels that bridge producers, traders, and buyers in these marketplaces and their consumers in their towns. Instant messaging applications on cell phones allow buyers to make advance orders to producers/traders and to send pictures of clothes they find during their visits to these marketplaces to prospective buyers, ensuring that the pieces they buy in La Salada and Feira da Madrugada will find final consumers. These apps have also increased the opportunities for drivers, guides, workers in bus transportation companies, and local porters. They can now receive consumer orders and proxy-buy goods in exchange for a commission. We have observed an increase in online sales of basic garments like tops, T-shirts, and bodysuits in the past years. However, many traders assert that understanding current fashion trends still requires physical presence and interaction within marketplaces and thousands of buyers still go to these markets.

The garment trade in La Salada and Feira da Madrugada takes place in small stalls where clothes hang in racks, are displayed in mannequins, or are placed over counters. Mannequins are much appreciated to indicate how clothes, and especially pants, would fit in customers' bodies. But the way these stalls are spatially organized is slightly different due to the areas where they are located.

La Salada marketplace and Feira da Madrugada are notable for their nighttime hours. Although unusual, this feature should not draw attention to itself. The decision to open the doors of the marketplaces at night has a double purpose. On the one hand, it seeks to reduce competition by taking advantage of a time slot when the rest of the shops close their doors. On the other hand, the preference for opening at night or in the early morning hours is intended to provide convenient hours for those who travel long distances. In any case, the opening hours and days change periodically according to the needs of demand or the opening strategies of the organizers.

What is known as the La Salada marketplace is three large indoor shed markets that house 8,000 stalls of garments spread over an area of 20 hectares. Each shed market has a parking lot where about 200 long-distance buses park daily. These buses bring shoppers from all over the country to stock up on garments, which they resell in their communities. In addition, each shed market has stalls rented out to garment entrepreneurs who arrive in their vehicles. This means that the main business of those who manage the shed markets is real estate, not selling clothes.

The influx of informal workshop producers generated informal employment opportunities for young men willing to transport large bags of garments from the producers' vehicles to the stalls located within shed markets or street markets. The emergence of a transportation system reliant on cart pullers occurred between 2001 and 2003 within the context of La Salada. The introduction of the cart-puller role was directly linked to the managers' desire to have a sizable workforce of young men working in the shed markets. These groups of cart-pullers have performed various functions, with the most visible being the transportation of substantial quantities of garments to and from the stalls in exchange for a negotiable fee. Notably, only the limited team of cart-pullers assigned by each shed market is authorized to provide this service of bringing garment bags into the shed markets. However, for each manager, the significance of these cart-puller groups extends beyond mere transportation. Through these young men, managers can exercise more effective control over the boundaries of each shed market, thereby enhancing security for the entrepreneurs who rent stalls inside.

Feira da Madrugada assumed over the years several material forms, from long corridors of stalls placed in the streets of Brás during the night hours to the currently scattered landscape that involves multistory buildings of different sizes and the streets. It now spreads over the best part of Brás (map 1). The area of the railroad depot also changed from a self-organized, informal, and open market that illegally occupied public land to a covered one-story building built by the Municipal Government with thousands of stalls licensed to vendors in colored sectors and now a multistory "shopping center" with 400 stalls, 315 parking slots for buses, and 2,400 parking slots for cars.[2] This place operates from 3 am until 4 pm daily except for Sundays. Initially, the term "Feira da Madrugada" exclusively referred to the activities in the derelict railroad depot, but it eventually came to represent the entire collection of commercial spaces selling clothes during the night. The marketplace inside the depot is currently complemented by many empty industrial buildings that were transformed into privately owned commercial galleries with small stalls with similar opening hours and streets. Figure 2 shows mannequins in front of stalls at one of the numerous shopping centers in Feira da Madrugada. These privately owned spaces follow a now widespread Chinese model for commercial spaces. Some of them are owned by Chinese descendants that accumulated capital using connections with producers and traders from the place of origin of their ancestors to promote circuits for the import of Chinese goods and controlling the space for their trade (Silva 2014). They have not replaced local production with imported clothes from Mainland China but retain significant power over real estate in the area. Most vendors in these spaces now have a tax registration number as "individual microentrepreneurs." They must collect a lump sum as tax and social security contributions, which not all of them regularly do.[3]

---

[2] These are numbers provided by the firm that manages the space and corresponds to the project. They can be found here: https://www.novafeiradamadrugada.com.br/feira-da-madrugada.html. Access on February 2, 2023.

[3] Individual microentrepreneurs (IME) were created and regulated in 2006 by Complementary Law 123/2006.

Figure 2 Mannequins in front of stalls at one of the numerous "shopping centers" that comprise Feira da Madrugada

Thousands of vendors continue competing for small spaces in the streets and sidewalks, taking shifts from the first hours of the day until the early morning hours. These spaces are organized by self-presented traders' association representatives charging for space, electricity, and protection. The municipal administration and police agents tolerate this irregular land use. But forbearance by law enforcers in the streets has a temporary limit: the opening times of formal shops. Vendors can still place stalls on the sidewalks, but police agents walk by the streets, forcing vendors to empty the streets early in the morning. Figure 3 shows one of the busy streets during the night at Feira da Madrugada.

The space itself is organized in a way that indicates differences in product quality to many of its visitors. The streets feature cheaper clothing options, either locally produced or imported. Some malls and galleries also aim to specialize in more affordable pieces. However, others have created more organized, spacious, and modern spaces, focusing on selling goods recognized for

Figure 3 One of the busy streets during the night at Feira da Madrugada

their higher quality. Once again, this is a viewpoint that many consumers often replicate. There are also highly sought-after niches, such as evangelical fashion, sportswear made from synthetic fabrics imported from China, and the so-called "plus-size" fashion, catering to larger sizes. This spatial specialization serves as a signaling system for buyers, which brings us to their activities.

Mirroring developments in Feira da Madrugada, entrepreneurs collaborated with influential local politicians from Lomas de Zamora to build a large shopping mall named "La Gran Dulce" across the River Matanza, a few blocks from the La Salada sheds. This project has been a political promise by Peronist politicians to producer-vendors and presented as an alternative to the informal management of La Salada, which has been the target of law enforcement (Olivera 2023). This recent development, threatened by the national political context, indicates changing political strategies and responses to these circuits, as well as the varying roles played by brokers and political intermediaries. We will further explore this theme in Section 5.

4 The Supply of Low-Cost Fashion: Creativity and Informal Entrepreneurship

"This is the item I sell the most during summertime," Leo said in La Salada, holding a child's cap aloft in the winter sun. "It's the one that sells the most," he insisted again and although we already knew each other quite well by that point, Leo suddenly adopted a new posture, as if he were about to explain the virtues of a new wonder product to a potential client at a trade fair. The small cap still in his hand, he continued to monitor the customers passing the stall while launching into an explanation of the development of his star product:

> When I started manufacturing this model, I used the cardboard visor – Papitex, the product's called. It's made of cardboard. It's a rubberized cardboard that doesn't get deformed when it comes in contact with water. But the visor's rigid; that's the problem. You want to give it a curved shape, which is what people like most, and you can't do that because it can break. You just can't. (Dewey 2020a, 121)

A crucial difference between both markets, La Salada and Feira da Madrugada, and the constellation depicted in the global value chain approach to economic development must be seen in the distinction between two different types of production units or sweatshops. The first type of production unit is the sweatshop, characteristic of global value chain literature. These are informal workshops linked to multinational companies or well-known retailers through subcontracting chains. Here, companies outsource specific mechanical or repetitive processes and keep the creative stage of garment production for themselves. The companies that outsource intensive labor are in charge of the design, derived from knowing their consumers while they are in contact with the consumers. In contrast, sweatshops are located upstream in the production chain. The second type of production unit, which is at the center of La Salada and Feira da Madrugada, is characterized by being concerned with design and creative tasks and outsourcing part of the production process to other workshops. In other words, these entrepreneurs identify their businesses as behaving like garment retailers, designing close to the consumers, and outsourcing tasks such as sewing, buttonholing, or ironing.

The paragraphs quoted at the beginning of this section are examples of how the workshops that supply garments in Argentina and Brazil differ from the classic upstream workshop tasked with repetitive, uncreative work. In Argentina and Brazil, informal garment entrepreneurs are engaged instead in producing garments tailored to buyers' preferences and needs. These entrepreneurs do not aim to provide mechanized services to other well-established firms. On the contrary, what defines the downstream position in countries is their frequent contact with buyers and the need to sound out their or other potential buyers' wishes. Crucially, this downstream position affects not only the commercialization chain, which is shortened but the entire production process. Being in contact with buyers implies an interest on the part of the entrepreneurs to adapt garments' design to the preferences, desires, or, more generally, the cultural representations of buyers. This downstream position, therefore, means that the work is organized "backward," starting from design choices made by the entrepreneurs. No less critical, such downstream position, that is, their proximity to the buyers, makes it possible to eliminate intermediaries and offer more competitive prices. This cost reduction, facilitated by marketplaces serving as meeting points for producers and buyers, is one of the key elements that explain the speed with which this economy has expanded. Entrepreneurs concentrate on a few products in the garment segment, and once the set of products for the new season is defined, the business is one of scale, a constellation that resembles Piore and Sabel's (1984) "flexibly specialized industrial districts" in which small firms specialize in the production of a limited range of products, while competing and being interrelated.

The division of labor described previously is aimed at producing "modinha," the specific form of fashion we described in the demand section. Modinha pieces are "made quickly, usually idealized and produced within a week, with quality and low price, and which, even with a certain concern for design, is usually the result of a replica, and is produced for wholesale at marketplaces" (Calíope and Silva Filho 2019, 143). In the context of these markets, as this description of "modinha" production indicates, copying is not an alien phenomenon in garment production processes. However, the evidence collected in Argentina and Brazil points to a process of copying that involves creativity and therefore challenges common assumptions about "copying" or "counterfeiting." Imitation of models is an inherent aspect of modinha production, but the proliferation of similar products leads to intense competition. As a result, they are compelled to engage in constant innovation to distinguish themselves and strive for excellence in the market. Figure 4 shows one of the numerous workshops that produce clothes sold at La Salada.

The practices described in this Element are often associated with the trade of "counterfeit" or trademark-infringing garments. In line with the global value chain approach, which typically associates creativity with well-known companies, the production of clothes for wholesale in La Salada and Feira da Madrugada are not usually considered sources of creativity. This is also reflected in the studies on upgrading where, with only a few exceptions (Aspers 2010a, 2010b), informal economies are not considered. One could speculate that upgrading literature does not look at these economies because it

Figure 4 One of the numerous workshops that produce clothes sold at La Salada

is assumed that work processes in informal workshops only involve copying. This lack of attention to creative processes contrasts with the interest in disciplines such as anthropology in cognitive, cultural, political, and legal aspects existing behind processes of imitation, copying, or counterfeiting (Boon 2010; Coombe 1993; Lempert 2014; Luvaas 2013; Manning 2010; Nakassis 2012; Raustiala and Sprigman 2012). Even this literature does not observe entrepreneurs' decisions as part of a pursuit of higher profit margins and based on continuous learning from buyers. In line with Vereta-Nahoum's (2021) findings about "modinha" in Feira da Madrugada, Dewey (2020b) shows that most of the garments sold in La Salada cannot be defined as "falsifications," that is, replicas of originals, but as garments inspired by recognized brand-name garments. Replicas are generally not sold in either marketplace, except for items like soccer T-shirts and athletic outfits whose value specifically depends on being replicas. This inspiration does not exclude the fraudulent use of brand logos but indicates that the business does not consist of simply copying. On the contrary, entrepreneurs use molds, colors, and designs of other garments – with proven success – as a reference and then include variations originating from dialogues, suggestions, or customer requests.

It is often a commercial advantage to copy some feature of another well-known garment. However, there are times when this is not the case. For example, one of the authors saw this when he was at Paulo's stand in La Salada. In the past, Paulo used to sell children's caps with the Nike swoosh on the front. However, driven by his desire to sell his designs, Paulo began to stop making products featuring the Nike Swoosh. Simultaneously, through contact with buyers, Paulo discovered that his buyers were not asking for the Nike swoosh but other details. As a result of this learning process, Paulo could finally redirect his efforts and resources to developing his products. This does not mean that Paulo has eliminated the Nike swoosh, but it does mean that his product portfolio has been diversified thanks to a learning process that is not at all different from the one that well-known companies go through.

In the context of La Salada and Feira da Madrugada, product portfolio diversification is widespread. Some producers sell "Adidas" jackets or pants, leggings, and T-shirts without brand names or logos. Others sell aprons with Disney images and plain aprons for professionals such as doctors or teachers. Still, others have developed their brand and sell products specifically tailored to buyers' needs, as with about half of the garments sold at La Salada. In Feira da Madrugada, branding is residual, and vendors have also developed niches: plus-sized clothes, modest fashion for Neopentecostal women, denim trousers, and seasonal pieces (jackets during winter and shorts during summer). This particular form of fashion might resemble essential fast fashion brands but bears no brands. If we accept that what downstream entrepreneurs do is also upgrading, that is, "transforming inputs into products more efficiently through reorganizing production or using superior technology" (Armando et al. 2016), then it can be argued that upgrading through design or copying in La Salada and Feira da Madrugada depends on different evaluation and decision-making processes. The concrete form that upgrading will take in the context of these economies results from a thorough evaluation of what will be in fashion in the next season and more subjective issues such as buyers' expectations. In addition to aesthetic considerations, other economic factors are also considered. For example, the cost of renting the stand depends on its location, the decision on the type of products (which affects the amount of fabric to be purchased), and other risks.

Another interesting aspect of the marketplaces dedicated to selling *modinha*, such as La Salada and Feira da Madrugada, is that the upgrading practices are not necessarily linked to the usual fashion cycles. The fact that entrepreneurs do not produce exact copies indicates that these production processes resemble the formal garment market only when brand logos are copied. This makes it clear that these two circuits do not necessarily reproduce the formal fashion industry internally in terms of cycles or content (colors, images, patterns, etc.). This decoupling between the markets is due, on the one hand, to the fact that the products are aimed at a broad but particular public (which is looking for a combination of affordable prices and "fashion") and, on the other hand, to the information-gathering practices developed by the entrepreneurs. Every market day, they listen to and interpret the demands of their customers and imagine their points of view. In other words, the entrepreneurs' work consists of imagining the performance of the goods (Beckert and Aspers 2011) and trying to decipher the buyers' imaginations.

The fashion input, the real difference between the two production processes mentioned previously, occurs toward the end of the manufacturing process. It is not a simple decorative task, but the moment of upgrading and involves a series of coordination tasks between the workshop and the environment (Aspers 2010; Evans and Smith 2006; Tokatli 2007, 2013). The empirical evidence collected in the workshops and interviews conducted in the context of La Salada shows that the entrepreneurs make a sustained effort to find inspiration in a number of sources of information, such as contact with customers, observation of competitors, products seen on the internet or in other shops, or simply communication within the family.

Leo's story, described at the beginning of this section, shows that the interpretation of buyers' behavior has real consequences on the work process within the workshop. Considering buyers' aesthetic orientations influences the coordination of tasks in each production unit. The fact that the customer demands a product with specific characteristics means that Leo has to carry out a series of actions. On the one hand, he has to find a source of funding for product improvements, such as the plastic visor that replaced the cardboard visor; and on the other, he has to decide who to subcontract the work to; he has to calculate the set of production and transport costs, as well as the times for each of these phases; finally, he has to redefine the quantities and qualities of fabric required for the new cap model.

Also, producing garments featuring famous brands' logos involves a series of decisions. These involve the very act of copying a product and everyday tasks in garment workshops. In any case, it is essential to emphasize that we are dealing with a specific mode of production: the production of brand-inspired fast-fashion, low-cost, flexibly ordered and delivered "just in time." One could argue that production units have internalized the dynamics of fast-fashion global supply chains, making Chu's analysis particularly relevant: "Its emphasis on the cyclical and rapid delivery of trendy, low-priced clothing necessitates a craft-based organization of garment production. More specifically, the assembly lines characteristic of the Fordist industrial model are fragmented, so only one specialized aspect of mass manufacture occurs within a single factory along the larger commodity chain" (Chu 2016, 195). However, local entrepreneurs replace foreign designer firms, making the decisions and subcontracting other workshops where repetitive tasks are performed. To inform these decisions, it is essential to monitor trends and preferences through constant dialogue with wholesale buyers and competitors, which we will now examine.

Monitoring

La Salada and Feira da Madrugada marketplaces receive thousands of visitors each day, and the thousands of stalls compete for the constant flow of customers walking the aisles interested in specific brands, qualities, prices, colors, quantities, delivery times, or shipment of garments. For these visitors, who buy in bulk with specific customers in mind, small details in the garments can mean the difference between stopping to talk to the vendor and continuing in search of the desired design. For example, during fieldwork in La Salada, entrepreneurs were explicit about the differences in using different brand logos. Some companies are more desirable than others, and entrepreneurs' task is to understand the customers, usually located in other provinces, of the buyers who visit the market. What wholesale buyers expect is communicated in short encounters where they feel the texture of the fabric, check the stitching, or look at the quality of the brand logos. Understanding the chain of expectations and preferences is part of the entrepreneurs' learning process, which is repeated continuously, forcing entrepreneurs to improve their products by changing the production process. Entrepreneurs are forced to overcome specific production problems to end up with fashionable products. Being "successful" in this business, therefore, means being able to understand the desires, expectations, and behaviors of customers and being able to adapt production to produce the desired garment.

However, this begs the question of what it means for producers to create "fashionable" garments. What are the parameters they consider if their job is not simply to copy? What do they do to determine the following trends, or simply what colors or designs will be "successful"? "Modinha" is the result of a series of practices whose purpose is quickly identifying opportunities, organizing production, testing products in the markets, and then reorganizing production to focus on the successful pieces. Conversely, being unable to interpret what customers want or learn from how they behave increases the likelihood of failing. In this sense, the circuits around La Salada and Feira da Madrugada are a graveyard of businesses that have failed because they have misinterpreted what colors and fabrics will be in demand in a season or what type of garment will be the best seller. One of the most important practices is to keep monitoring the marketplace. Monitoring consists of a set of practices whose primary purpose is information gathering. The decisions that entrepreneurs make and whether they are successful depend on the quality and quantity of the information they can gather. A definite interpretation of "what clothes consumers want to buy" is the sum of the collected information.

The first type of monitoring practice that entrepreneurs engage in is "walking the marketplace," which consists of walking the aisles of the marketplace to gather information about what is being sold, what the garments they plan to produce look like, and, of course, to check prices. The second set of practices occurs outside the marketplace and focuses on two information sources: the internet and the fabric store. The internet is used to check models, colors, shapes, and other relevant information through various applications such as Facebook or Instagram. On the other hand, the fabric shop is where the entrepreneur meets the fabric seller, who is usually an expert and has a good knowledge of the colors that will be used in the coming season. In both cases, these are sources of information that have a fundamental impact on the decisions made by the entrepreneurs. The third monitoring practice that entrepreneurs constantly carry out is checking the garments' prices displayed in the same marketplace. In both La Salada and Feira da Madrugada, entrepreneurs sell low-priced garments, which is a business characteristic. Therefore, price monitoring leads entrepreneurs to adapt to the prevailing prices. Price monitoring allows for correcting wrong decisions in many cases. The fourth practice of monitoring is to pay attention to what the customers are communicating to them. Therefore, an important parameter is the opinion of buyers together with the production of small batches of clothing, the latter also allowing to avoid significant losses in case of a wrong decision.

Informality in La Salada and Feira da Madrugada

We have argued that the production, trade, and distribution of clothes surrounding La Salada and Feira da Madrugada involve various degrees and forms of informality, which partially accounts for the price competitiveness of their garments. The monotributo and MEI systems have contributed to the formalization of some businesses within these circuits. However, the realm of production, characterized by activities fragmented across vast networks of subcontracting producers and shops, remains informal to a large degree. But in what sense do we use the term "informal"?

There is a broad scholarly consensus that informality is a dynamic process rather than a static duality (Davis 2017; Boudreau and Davis 2017; Guha-Khasnobis, Kanbur, and Ostrom 2006; Meagher 2016, 2013). Under this premise, this study proposes that legal definitions should be taken seriously, as they determine a large part of the social dynamics observed in these circuits. Legal definitions are relevant because they force people to behave in specific ways. They determine access to credit or the location of firms in the urban space; they impact the possibility of using specific infrastructures and the safety of workers;

or they are crucial for understanding the growth of particular firms and the failure of others. At the most general level, legal definitions, which express specific struggles of interests, are how the state tries to impose a legal order (Weber 1978). By defining social phenomena in a particular way and providing the means to enforce the rules, the state seeks to impose a legal order which competes with other conceptions of order.

On the contrary, to ignore legal definitions would be to lose the possibility of appreciating the failure or success associated with states' attempts to formalize the economies in question; to appreciate the strategies used by actors to evade or break the rules, and, finally, to understand how government or state agents negotiate the terms of the law with representatives of these economies. What does informal or illegal mean in these economies? There are no simple answers to this question but from the actors involved in the production and distribution stages, noncompliance with regulations is a way of reducing costs to be competitive. We can observe informality in the production and commercialization processes.

In the circuits analyzed in this study, garment production is carried out in at least two types of productive units: some dedicated to the design, cutting, and finishing of garments and others dedicated to mechanical tasks such as sewing, buttonholing, or gluing labels. In these two productive units, formal or informal means meeting (or not meeting) formal requirements in at least three dimensions (Tokman 1992). The first relates to obtaining legal authorization for these units to be part of the formal economy. In most cases, this involves a registration process and compliance with health and safety requirements, sometimes subject to official inspections. This is the case for workshops where workers must use machinery, or the work process may affect workers' health. The second dimension relates to taxes, the payment of which implies that the representatives of the productive units have registered as taxpayers. Being formal from a tax point of view means registering and paying taxes continuously. Finally, the third dimension refers to the relationship between the economic unit and the workers. This includes the registration of workers, the payment of wages and social security contributions according to the regulations in force, and the recognition of their rights. Although the distinction between informal and formal is conceptually straightforward, the social reality is far more complex. Empirical evidence shows that most cases are not at the extremes but in the middle of a continuum. However, having clarified that gray areas prevail, it is essential to note that the empirical evidence collected shows that informality is exceptionally high compared to formal productive units in the sector.

In Argentina and Brazil, there are policy instruments aimed at the formalization of producers and traders and which are employed by production units and traders in La Salada and Feira da Madrugada. In Argentina, people can apply for the so-called monotributo. It is a simplified tax regime for small taxpayers aiming to facilitate the payment of tax obligations without the need to file tax returns. It is a legal instrument widely used by garment producers and vendors in La Salada. However, registering as a single taxpayer is not enough when the manufacturing units cease to be sole proprietorships and begin to have employees. In these cases, the Labor Code requires the employer to register employees and comply with additional obligations. The interviews conducted and the visits to the workshops reveal a landscape in which the use of the individual taxpayer is common, but not the formal registration of employees or the authorization of production units to operate as such. This is without considering that a common practice, as described, is the informal subcontracting of other informal workshops to carry out tasks such as sewing, ironing, or buttonholing.

The situation in Brazil is similar, although the instrument used, the so-called "MEI" (Individual Microentrepreneur), is slightly broader than the "monotributo" as it allows the "microentrepreneur" to have one employee without any additional formalities. Opening a formal business, whether as a MEI or in another legal form, also requires municipal authorization. In other words, to formally incorporate a firm, the entrepreneur must comply with municipal legislation and take care of the final authorization. The municipal authorities will evaluate whether the company's location corresponds to the urban zoning, whether it meets the health requirements, and so on. As Carlos Freire points out, with similarities to the Argentine case, "this is precisely where the division between those who can be formalized and those who cannot is at work" (Silva 2014, 85). Despite successive waves of simplification (Vereta-Nahoum 2019) aiming at fostering the formalization and regularization of informal production and trade in Brazil, the two main legal instruments aimed at formalizing traders – the MEI tax and social security regime and the land-use permits, for those aiming at working in the streets – continue to require some degree of knowledge of bureaucratic meanders, which sometimes act as a hindrance and limits the reach of the formalization policies.

In short, in both countries, we observe instruments that seek to formalize workers and provide them with social security benefits but are better adapted to the needs and activities of vendors than garment entrepreneurs' needs in the production stage. The Brazilian figures for MEI are particularly revealing. Among the various occupations, traders of garments stand out as the second-largest group of MEIs, comprising 1,005,329 individual entrepreneurs as of June 2023. Notably, the city of São Paulo boasts a substantial number, with

69,490 garment traders opting to operate under the MEI regime. In contrast, the total count of clothing producers and confection service providers in Brazil that operate as MEI amounts to 174,896, whereas in the city of São Paulo, it reaches 18,036.[4]

Finally, it is worth highlighting some practices different from tax evasion or official controls and usually defined as illegal. In production, the fraudulent use of well-known brand logos is widespread. This is done with the producers' justification that it will increase sales. Although producers often do not make exact copies or replicas but creative ones (Dewey 2020a, 2020b), the sheer use of brand logos violates trademark laws. As explained next concerning the La Salada marketplace, this massive transgression has incentivized various actors, including provincial and national security forces, to collect protection rackets systematically. The other set of practices, now in the realm of commercialization, refers to garment vendors' occupation of public space. In both marketplaces, the occupation of streets or sidewalks has led to various government responses, ranging from tolerance to attempted relocation to eviction.

In this Element, we use terms such as "informal workshop" and "informal production unit" or use the adjective "illegal" to refer to phenomena derived from legal definitions. This is not to criminalize, as some might argue, but to highlight the interactions of agents when a legal order seeks to compete with other conceptions of order and their parallel obligations and costs. By taking legal definitions seriously, we can expand our knowledge of how the state sees these economic contexts (Scott 1998). State laws and procedures oblige people to make decisions, that is, to comply (or not) with them. Rule takers may follow the rules, discover their limitations, manipulate them, or ignore them altogether.

Meanwhile, rule givers want to establish a particular order, usually called "formalization." However, they may also be interested in creating unconducive rules, refusing to enforce the law, or prioritizing the formalization of specific social segments or economic sectors to the detriment of others. This involves specific practices, decisions, and sociologically relevant knowledge amid a continuum of gray areas. In the following section we discuss how state agencies and politicians have seen, reacted, and intervened in Feira da Madrugada and La Salada across time.

---

[4] The data on MEI is provided by the Entrepreneur Portal of the Ministry of Finance of Brazil. It can be found here: http://www22.receita.fazenda.gov.br/inscricaomei/private/pages/relatorios/opcoesRelatorio.jsf. Access on July 27, 2023. The figures exclude the production of custom-made garments.

5 State and Governments' Responses

The Feira da Madrugada and La Salada were established and thrived over the years, thanks to the efforts of producer-vendors, local brokers, and specific socioeconomic conditions. These informal marketplaces may appear to be the result of spontaneous self-organization. However, it is essential to acknowledge that political efforts or at least tolerance have also played a crucial role in their survival, as these informal marketplaces often involve irregular use of land, tax evasion, and other violations of the law, which could potentially lead to their closure and the sanctioning of their vendors. Moreover, their operation depends on infrastructures provided directly or indirectly by public administrations, sometimes through political intermediaries, necessitating a political construction that ranges from forbearance to formalization attempts.

Policies targeting the consumption of low-income individuals have been instrumental in both Argentina and Brazil. Additionally, local politics and their attitudes toward informal commerce and urban retail spaces have significantly influenced the trajectory of these marketplaces, albeit in different ways for La Salada and Feira da Madrugada. The reactions and interactions with government officers, law enforcers, politicians, and party agents have all played a part in shaping these marketplaces. Intense political debates in town halls have further amplified opposing views on the fate of these markets, with some politicians denouncing illegalities of their activities and advocating for their closure, while others recognize their social and economic significance for families, cities, and the countries, and argue for their preservation, seeking political support from those who benefit from such practices.

In common, the dominant attitudes in both marketplaces have evolved from a mixture of repression aiming at their disappearance and extortion to a proactive attempt to legitimize their activities, with or without ongoing forbearance. In recent years, politicians in Argentina and Brazil have expressed legitimating discourses to justify these marketplaces, acknowledging the economic possibilities of activities previously considered backward and precarious. Discourses of the latter type have been more strongly associated with the Workers' Party in São Paulo and the Justicialista Party in Greater Buenos Aires, but Radicales councilors (members of the Unión Cívica Radical party) have also played a role as political intermediaries of beneficial policies toward La Salada. These discourses are often connected with the promotion of petty entrepreneurship and the creation of particular legal forms to foster the formalization of trade: the individual microentrepreneur (MEI), in Brazil, and the "monotributista," in Argentina. Formalization and the resort to private solutions for the organization of the marketplace have been more central to the Brazilian strategies, and, as such, brokers at the meso level remain more active in the Argentine case.

In the following analysis, we explore four reactions that governments in Brazil and Argentina have employed over the years: repression, extortion, forbearance, and formalization. Given the widespread informality involved in these economies and its crucial role in keeping production and distribution costs down, however, we put more attention to forbearance as a governmental strategy to cope with and even enhance these fashion circuits. We demonstrate that the successful persistence of these economies hinges on a combination of forbearance and attempts at formalization.

Demonization and Repression of Commercial Activities

The marketplaces of La Salada and Feira da Madrugada have been the subject of contentious public and political debates. Over time, politicians, law enforcement agents, representatives of shop owners, and segments of society have expressed concerns regarding the illegal activities, perceived uncleanliness, and potential risks posed to consumers in these marketplaces. These criticisms have been accompanied by efforts to shut down the marketplaces and seize their goods.

The production, trade, and distribution of low-income clothes in these marketplaces involve various aspects of informality and illegality, including the irregular use of public land. These activities have contributed to the stigmatization and resistance toward La Salada and Feira da Madrugada, especially considering that the sellers often come from socially disadvantaged segments of Argentine and Brazilian societies, including recent migrants.

For instance, the Feira da Madrugada first gained attention and became a subject of debate at São Paulo's Town Hall in 2006, with calls for dismantling the stalls and suppressing the commercial activities perceived as problematic for the area. The marketplace continued to be a matter of concern and debate at town hall sessions until 2018, when construction for a new shopping center at the Pari railroad depot began under private concession. Over this period, the São Paulo Municipal Official Bulletin featured 661 mentions of the area, encompassing normative acts, executive decisions, and numerous speeches by city councilors.[5] The issue of street commerce in the region remains a matter of ongoing concern and discussion to this day.

---

[5] The search was conducted at the online version of the *Bulletin*, covering the period January 2005 to April 2018, employing the expression "Feira da Madrugada" in quotation marks. The results can be checked here: http://www.docidadesp.imprensaoficial.com.br/ResultadoBusca.aspx?PalavraChave=Feira%20da%20Madrugada&GrupoCaderno=Cidade%20de%20SP;&DtIni=2/1/2005&DtFim=30/04/2018.

During its first years, the activities at the Feira da Madrugada were invariably portrayed as "illegal." This alleged illegality involved multiple dimensions: the unauthorized use of public land, sale of counterfeit and smuggled goods, and other irregularities. The cover of the *São Paulo Municipal Bulletin* on February 14, 2006, informed about a "true illegal Night Market that has been set up in the past five years without authorization" (DOCSP 2006). The municipal administration saw repressing what was essentially street commerce as essential to protect formal garment stores and employment from what they perceived as "unfair competition" and to suppress criminal activities that may arise. In other words, these activities were repressed on the grounds that it harmed employment and income. In 2007, councilors, notably Adilson Amadeu, who represented store owners in the area, publicly voiced their concerns about the sale of counterfeit and smuggled goods in the marketplace and called for law enforcement action (DOCSP 2008a). For many years, police and municipal law enforcers carried out frequent and often sensationalized raids against traders, accompanied by media reporters and involving prominent members of the municipal administration, including the mayor (DOCSP 2007).

Following the relocation of the Feira da Madrugada to the abandoned railroad depot, public and political attention shifted to the irregular organization of the public land and the distribution of stalls. Mr. Amadeu publicly condemned the irregular use of land and the sale of illegal goods in the depot on multiple occasions. As a response, the municipal and state administrations continued to resort to dramatic police raids, seizing goods, and, at times, leading to temporary closures of the space. Conflicts over the control of the space and the organization of activities involved various public and private actors, as well as individuals purporting to represent vendors, leading to increased public attention and criticism directed toward the marketplace. Even the concession of the Pari Depot, discussed further in the section dedicated to formalization attempts, faced controversy and criticism from politicians and trader associations, who perceived the concession as a loss of their power to control the space and trade stalls. A Parliamentary Inquiry Committee (CPI) at São Paulo's City Council was formed to investigate the conditions of the concession from June to December 2017, resulting in specific recommendations that recognized the consortium that won the bidding process (Vereta-Nahoum 2019).

Given that repression was the main public attitude of the local government toward the marketplace, Feira da Madrugada operated during its earlier years through a combination of extortion from local officials responsible for street regulation and the leniency of police forces, who often turned a blind eye

(G1 2008). In the face of such policies, extortion by private associations and state agents played a crucial role in the persistence of these marketplaces.

Extortion

The continued existence of informal marketplaces like La Salada and Feira da Madrugada, despite operating in the gray area of informality and illegality, can be attributed, in part, to the practice of extortion by both state and private actors. The enforcement of laws is inherently discretionary, allowing State agents to choose whether to overlook violations or enforce them strictly. These agents can also manipulate the selective application or even suspension of law enforcement as leverage to gain political or economic advantages. They wield the power of legal coercion and the potential for proper enforcement as a political commodity, creating an asymmetrical bargaining position when negotiating with local producers and traders (Misse 2010). These negotiations often involve the exchange of monetary gains to inspectors or political favors, with politicians seeking support and votes from those involved in the marketplaces.

In both marketplaces, State agents are known to extort producers and traders, in the form of bribes and informal taxation. Investigations into Feira da Madrugada by journalists and politicians at Feira da Madrugada have revealed instances of officers from the local government and police agents demanding bribes from traders (see G1 2008, for example). Similarly, in La Salada, a corrupt system akin to a hidden tax has taken root. This system centers on informal entrepreneurs selling clothing items bearing famous brand logos, which infringe trademark laws. To avoid law enforcement, these entrepreneurs transfer money to local politicians in exchange for the non-enforcement of laws. This arrangement is mutually beneficial, as producers rely on selling garments with recognizable brand logos, while local politicians receive funds for their activities. The "fee," commonly known as "marca," is relatively low but consistently collected. Each time a stallholder displays clothes with logos in La Salada, they must pay the "marca" fee, and these transactions are meticulously recorded in accounting books. Based on estimates derived from a survey of the number of stalls offering "branded" garments (around 40–60 percent of the total 8,000 stalls), the monthly collection from this system amounts to approximately US$770,000.

In the case of Feira da Madrugada, certain private groups masquerading as traders' associations exert coercion on street traders. They offer protection against law enforcement in exchange for payment for renting spaces in the streets, as well as lighting and general security services. Before the concession of the Pari Depot, these groups also controlled the allocation and trading of stalls within the marketplace and acted as protection rackets against law enforcement. In 2010, the Municipality of Sao Paulo took control of the area in an agreement with the Federal government, its rightful owner. A Managing Committee, led by retired police officers, was established to oversee the distribution of stalls. However, both the Committee and local associations were later found to be involved in the illicit trade of stalls, issuing permits for new stall construction and alterations to existing ones. In 2012, a newspaper article exposed that new stalls were being traded for exorbitant sums, up to 500,000 Brazilian Reais (approximately US$250,000 at the exchange rates of that time), with bribes paid to the Managing Committee and a local association in the area (ESTADO 2012). Two years prior to this, the Municipal administration had already recognized the market's infiltration by a stall trading system and had issued an ordinance prohibiting any charges for occupying the area.[6]

Forbearance

Another dimension of the selective enforcement of laws or its suspension by state agents is forbearance. Forbearance materializes through the suspension of the enforcement of various types of laws or the creation of regulations that facilitate or even encourage the violation of norms. Not all discretionary application of regulations is tied to economic gains for enforcers; it can equally indicate an underlying political support for certain practices. Recent analyses, highlighting the role of government forbearance in the face of regulatory violations (Dewey 2017; Dewey and Di Carlo 2022; Gordon and Hafer 2013; Holland 2017), particularly in the region's informal economies, demonstrate that non-enforcement of regulations at the subnational and national levels plays a fundamental role in fostering economic activity and political stability.

The governments in the studied region have traditionally benefited from the economic circuits centered around La Salada and Feira da Madrugada by harnessing their dynamism, which allows them to provide economic opportunities for those excluded from the formal labor market and offer low-cost garments to low-income consumers. The fact that the informal sector provides an alternative to unemployment and offers affordable basic goods is undeniably attractive for governments that may lack the interest or means to change this reality. These markets have generated real income opportunities and, above all, have protected many local governments from social conflict and unrest, as evidenced by the informal work figures and biographical profiles described previously. They have also promoted consumption and, more fundamentally,

---

[6] PORTARIA INTERSECRETARIAL No 04/SMSP/SEMDET/2010.

provided clothing to sectors of the population that have limited access to garments sold by formal stores.

In the contexts studied here, regulatory forbearance can be observed in three areas: the absence of labor inspections, the lax enforcement of sales taxes, and tolerance toward the irregular use of streets and public land. Despite hundreds of thousands of producers and sellers working daily in the circuits centered around La Salada and Feira da Madrugada, labor inspections are either absent or, at best, selective in both marketplaces. In the Argentine case, the responsibility for labor regulation is shared between the National and Provincial governments. The Ministry of Labor enforces the registration of workers in the social security system and, in collaboration with the tax agency, ensures the payment of payroll taxes. On the other hand, local governments are responsible for enforcing labor conditions. In the case of La Salada, this responsibility falls on the provincial government of Buenos Aires. However, neither the Federal nor provincial authorities actively pursue labor inspections. As a result, none of the approximately 200,000 workers in the region are formally registered, implying that they are excluded from access to contributory social security benefits, including health insurance.

In the case of the workshops producing clothes for Feira da Madrugada, labor regulations have been selectively enforced. Labor inspectors from the Ministry of Labor and labor prosecutors have focused on workshops that impose labor conditions similar to slavery, which is a criminal offense under the Brazilian Penal Code (article 149). These include forced labor, long working hours, degrading conditions, and restrictions on the movement of workers. During the 2010s, the garment industry was a major target of their oversight and enforcement activities, leading to media and public attention toward some of their supervision and "liberation" actions. In these actions, workers were freed, and workshops providing services to large retail groups were fined. In response to these actions, the Legislative Assembly of the State of Sao Paulo conducted a Parliamentary Inquiry Commission against slave labor in 2014 to investigate labor conditions in the industry and develop a plan to combat slave-like practices. Large clothing retail firms admitted to the lack of oversight of outsourced workshops and committed to taking corrective measures (Ojeda 2014).

The enforcement of regulations has been concentrated on abusive practices and often singled out workshops working for large retailers. The main strategy of inspectors and prosecutors has been to publicly shame these large groups in order to raise awareness among their consumers. However, the production of clothes in workshops for sale at the various venues encompassing Feira da

Madrugada, which operates outside the logic of outsourcing, has not received the same level of oversight or repression.

It is crucial to note that the production model adopted in Feira da Madrugada and La Salada, characterized by network arrangements where highly specialized garment workers and connected workshops contribute to the step-by-step on-demand production of clothes, often without contracts or subordination, blurs the line between workers and entrepreneurs. This situation creates confusion and poses challenges in enforcing labor regulations in La Salada and Feira da Madrugada. Categorizing this situation as forbearance is challenging because there is no clear understanding of how labor standards, designed to regulate formal employment, apply to these practices, which are considered self-employment by the producers. The labor practices are often autonomous networks of confection service providers receiving payment for their work and producers selling their output in these marketplaces. Additionally, many workers, including those in workshops, operate as individual entrepreneurs (monotributistas and MEIs).

Workshop owners also exploit this legal form, despite employing multiple workers, to evade labor regulations and employer obligations. This practice has not received significant attention from labor authorities, suggesting selective enforcement. However, many migrant workers in these regions have managed to climb what Benencia and Quaranta (2006) refer to as "the Bolivian ladder," in a study of migrant workers in Greater Buenos Aires involved in the production and trade of fresh produce. Social mobility is also evident in the garment industry in these contexts, as many workers who can access or buy sewing machines become autonomous producers selling their own production. At times, inspectors and prosecutors have targeted workshops, leading to resistance from producer-sellers who argue that local authorities fail to understand the collective and autonomous nature of their activities. Migrant workers from Andean countries have sought to express their culture as a means to reframe their image and counteract prejudices in Brazil and Argentina that associate them with appalling working conditions (Silva 2012).

At Feira da Madrugada, forbearance has predominantly been observed concerning irregular uses of space and taxation. Throughout the years, the trading activities in the area have been characterized by a complex politics of space (Vereta-Nahoum 2019), involving conflicting interests among private groups claiming to represent traders, police forces, municipal law enforcers, and politicians.

Law enforcement agencies have shown tolerance toward the illicit occupation of street spaces by private individuals who engage in extortion by charging vendors for the use of these spaces. Over time, the police have informally regulated the timing of occupation, allowing vendors to utilize the streets during the night until formal shops open. In conjunction with this leniency, local authorities have consistently viewed the construction of shopping centers as a means to regulate the unauthorized use of street space, formalize trade, and mitigate extortion by private individuals and law enforcement agents.

Authorities also demonstrate leniency toward the taxation of sales activities, even though many vendors, especially those operating in shopping centers and the "Circuito de Compras," are now individual microentrepreneurs (MEIs) who pay a lump sum for their trade. Another factor contributing to this forbearance is state taxation on the circulation of goods. Before a recent tax reform, Brazil imposed state-level taxes on the consumption of goods and services, and transportation of commercial goods across state borders was subject to inspections to ensure tax compliance. Intensified enforcement efforts on roads targeted resellers transporting goods without proper invoices, which helped reduce tax evasion to some extent. However, the fact that some resellers still prefer to transport goods on passenger buses to evade freight service requirements, which mandate showing invoices and declaring the value of the goods, suggests that there remains a significant level of forbearance by state tax authorities.

A dimension of regulatory forbearance that future research should consider is related to the use of payment methods developed by Central Banks and fintechs, specifically virtual wallets. These virtual wallets, such as Mercado Pago, PayPal, Tarjeta Ualá (in Argentina), PicPay, and Ame (in Brazil), have been developed under the auspices of governments and the narrative of "financial inclusion." They offer digital wallets and credit, operating similarly to banking products but subject to different regulations (BCRA 2022). In the Argentinian case, the regulation for opening an account and handling payments with digital wallets has been limited and lenient. In Brazil, the Central Bank introduced its own free digital means of payment called Pix to promote financial inclusion and reduce financial costs (BCB 2020).

The effects of these new means of payment seem paradoxical. On the one hand, they facilitate financial transactions in these marketplaces, increase payment security, reduce financial costs associated with card operators and card machines for traders, and enhance the legibility of informal activities, their transactions, and their size for state authorities. For instance, PIX in Brazil was explicitly designed as a system to reduce the potential for tax evasion and enhance payment security. The decrease in cash transactions in these marketplaces also contributes to reducing criminality, which has been a challenge faced by Feira da Madrugada over the years. Additionally, resellers mention that these payment methods facilitate transactions and prevent payment defaults, especially among neighbors and relatives, who are trusted individuals often deferring payments.

On the other hand, these new means of payment create new opportunities for producers and traders to receive large sums of money without paying taxes. Interviews with garment entrepreneurs illustrate this fact: production units manufacturing thousands of garments per week manage their finances using only virtual wallets. By utilizing various means, they disperse their income to take advantage of beneficial tax systems for individual entrepreneurs, presenting tax authorities with a fragmented view of their income.

Extortion and forbearance highlight the role of mediators at the meso level, bridging local agents in both markets and those in charge of law enforcement. These mediators not only organize extortion and collect fees, like the traders' associations and managers, but also negotiate the variable application of laws and regulations with politicians and state officials. The role of these representatives, operators, and associations is to broker agreements with friendly politicians in power. Regardless of their political allegiances or party lines, they have negotiated with elected councilors who recognize the economic and political benefits of tolerating informal activities in La Salada and Feira da Madrugada.

Explaining Forbearance: Forbearance as a Policy, Not a Sign of State Weakness

But why do police officers, state inspectors, and politicians choose to forbear in La Salada and Feira da Madrugada? This question suggests that law enforcement is more influenced by political strategies than by state capacity.

A common explanation for the lack of enforcement is the weakness of state institutions. However, there are instances where states considered "strong" fail to enforce the law in certain areas, and cases where supposedly "weak" states are capable of effective law enforcement. While lack of state capacity refers to structural impediments that the literature treats as more or less constant over time, variations in compliance suggest that the willingness to enforce the law may respond to changes in the government's political attitude. State capacity is not static, and there are numerous examples of supposedly weak states – such as Bangladesh, Paraguay, and Rwanda – that have successfully enhanced their state capacity to collect tax revenues through sustained political commitment and administrative reforms (OECD 2015).

Furthermore, explanations based on state capacity typically treat it as given "exogenously" and overlook the self-interested motivations of those political actors controlling the state (Acemoglu 2005). However, if we consider the self-interested motivations of rule-makers, it becomes clear that state weakness may be endogenous to politics (Besley & Persson 2009). This means that governments may intentionally undermine state capacity as part of their political strategy. In other words, governments have the legal authority to both strengthen and weaken state capabilities.

Taking heed of these criticisms, current studies analyze the lack of enforcement due to purposeful political agency. Thus, politicians' strategic law non-enforcement has been used to respond to increasing competitive pressures produced by trade opening (Ronconi 2012) or as a tool to extract resources from specific economic activities (Ceccagno 2017, 2024; Dewey 2018b, 2020a).[7] This perspective has gained momentum with Holland's (2016, 2017) work on forbearance. In her view, politicians capture enforcement agencies and use regulatory non-enforcement to redistribute benefits with the expectation of being rewarded by voters during elections. In line with previous work (Dewey and Di Carlo 2022), we extend Holland's electoral explanation in two ways. First, we highlight the economic logic of forbearance used for industrial policy motives rather than purely electoral ones.

If, with governments' connivance, tax regulations are enforced only for some producer groups, regions, or sectors but not for others, the latter de facto enjoy a tolerated exemption vis-à-vis other actors subjected to effective enforcement. Non-enforcement becomes selective because the possibility of avoiding regulation is not an equally viable option for all economic actors or sectors in the economic system. Selective tax non-enforcement jeopardizes compliance and reduces effective tax rates by facilitating tax evasion (Genschel and Schwarz 2011, 352). Tax evasion by some distorts market competition and undermines the principle of "horizontal tax equity," according to which taxpayers in similar circumstances should bear similar tax burdens (Feria 2020, 11). Fewer tax disbursements to the state lower the relative input costs, which the noncompliant producers face vis-à-vis the compliant ones. Thanks to relatively lower production costs, the noncompliant economic actors can make higher profits – which can be reinvested to increase one's competitiveness further – or pass part of the savings onto lower prices capturing market shares from those law-abiding competitors (Santiago 2010).

Therefore, forbearance is a functional equivalent to a fiscal subsidy, which can be targeted at "helping the losers" and "picking winners." In the former

---

[7] The intention to forbear informal and illegal behavior should be distinguished from what David Weil (2014) calls the "fissuring" of the employment relationship. It is not a process of splitting off or pushing outward of organizational functions that before were part of the big formal companies. The mushrooming of small productive units and small trade businesses emerges from entrepreneurs' identification of business opportunities. Moreover, Leo's business is not seeking to deliver services to other big companies.

sense, as we show in both cases, forbearance slows the process of creative destruction by granting less productive and less innovative undertakings, such as sweatshop-based garment production, a greater chance to survive than the one they would have in a regime of effective regulatory enforcement (Bobbio 2016). At the same time, forbearance may work as a pull mechanism that attracts would-be garment entrepreneurs within one's jurisdiction by promising a lax approach to enforcing costly regulations (Genschel and Schwarz 2011, 352). In both cases, forbearance tampers with the self-regulating mechanism of markets and alters the economy's structure.

This is evident in the circuits around Feira da Madrugada and La Salada. Weak state capacity does not account for forbearance in these cases, as police and inspectors have at times been able to repress activities and close stalls or even significant parts of these marketplaces. Forbearance is employed as a subtle mode of industrial policy.

This holds particular significance in an era when the conventional methods of state incentives toward industrial activities, previously embraced by both the Argentinian and Brazilian governments as part of their import substitution industrialization initiatives, have fallen out of favor among politicians and business representatives alike.

The Argentinian and Brazilian governments exploit the selective non-enforcement of economic regulations as a strategic means to govern the economy. By tinkering with enforcement mechanisms – that is, applying "political leniency" (Holland 2016, 233) or pursuing the "reduction in the stringency" and effectiveness of enforcement mechanisms (Gordon and Hafer 2013, 209) – governments at different levels confer selected advantages to targeted socioeconomic groups who benefit vis-à-vis other law-abiding market actors such as legal garment producers. Through fewer disbursements to the state, groups of noncompliers such as garment entrepreneurs, stallholders, or traders enjoy a combination of higher profits and the capacity to pass on part of such savings onto their final prices, capturing market shares from compliant competitors. Regulatory forbearance, therefore, can be thought of as functionally equivalent to a direct subsidy used as an instrument of industrial policy.

Forbearance becomes an attractive policy choice when governments want to aid thousands of garment entrepreneurs and traders scattered throughout national territories; or when the productive structure of the country is such, for instance, featuring high levels of labor informality, that regulatory forbearance can be deployed more effectively than alternative lawful industrial policies.

Public Legitimation and Formalization

The recognition of the importance of Feira da Madrugada and La Salada in generating income in urban decaying industrial zones for thousands and providing affordable clothes has led to not only selective enforcement or suspension of law enforcement but also to discourses and policies aiming at legitimizing producers and traders while reorganizing these marketplaces and their activities in formal ways. While some politicians argued for their closure, claiming they harmed employment and income, others contested this view, defending the rights of vendors and recognizing the economic significance of these activities for thousands of families (DOCSP 2008b, 2008c). Demonizing and legitimating discourses have always coexisted.

Authorities often grant official recognition and political support for these marketplaces in exchange for beneficial resources, such as suppressing protests by vendors and gaining political advantages from improved access to affordable clothing, informal jobs, and consumer goods for economically disadvantaged populations. In both cases, parties on the left of the political spectrum have shown friendlier and more supportive attitudes toward these marketplaces. Efforts toward formalization have been associated with the consolidation of these markets and a commitment by left-wing parties in Argentina (Peronism) and Brazil (the Workers' Party) to the importance of popular entrepreneurship and consumption, linked to political stability. For instance, in 2012, the Argentine president included Alejandro Morado, a second-in-command of a La Salada market shed, in her entourage to an official trip to promote trade relations with Angola, thus providing political validation to an economy characterized by informality and illegality.

On the one hand, authorities provide public legitimacy to influential actors in these markets, while on the other hand, they exploit the functioning of this economy. Guillermo Moreno, Argentina's former secretary of commerce, allegedly declared in public that "If it weren't for La Salada, our people would have no place to buy their clothes," according to one of his advisors interviewed by one of the authors.

These marketplaces also serve as a source of resources for local politicians in urgent situations. For instance, shed-market managers collected garments internally in 2013 for a government-run social program called "Ropa para Todos" (Clothing for Everyone), in which La Salada was intended to contribute by supplying garments. This program inadvertently sourced clothing from workshops that violated various standards, including labor standards. The existence of these informal practices alongside formalization attempts further emphasizes the complexity of the relationship between the market and the government.

The histories of Feira da Madrugada and La Salada reveal successive attempts by state agencies to formalize, organize, and control their activities based on their own visions of popular marketplaces. National and local policies have aimed at promoting formalization and consumption of clothes. This suggests that despite originally self-organized by vendors, many of which producers of clothes, Feira da Madrugada and La Salada were equally politically constructed.

This is particularly evident in the case of Feira da Madrugada, where formalization attempts have been more intense. Since its establishment, various state agencies, politicians, and law enforcement agents have made significant efforts to develop infrastructures that align with their vision of an appropriate "popular" marketplace (Vereta-Nahoum 2019). National politics played a minor direct role in the organization of this marketplace, but due to the Federal State's ownership of the railroad depot where the marketplace was located, it intervened at times.

In 2008, authorities shifted their attention to the irregular occupation of the depot. The initial calls for the closure of the large marketplace were gradually replaced by attempts to take control of the space and replace organizations that claimed to represent the vendors. The administration and the majority of counselors shifted their approach toward formalization and regulation. Feira da Madrugada has undergone successive interventions. In 2011, after newspapers exposed that the Ministry of Transportation had demanded bribes in a dubious agreement with a local manager to allow commercial activities in the depot (Magalhães 2011), the Federal government agreed to cede the management of the area to the Municipal government. A new management committee was established, comprising members of the Municipal administration and police officers. While the marketplace was initially organized, illicit trade and stall construction continued.

In 2013, a new Municipal administration constructed a large covered structure with thousands of equally sized stalls. The administration encouraged vendors to obtain permits and remain in the area, recognizing the significance of this economic activity. The new administration believed that Feira da Madrugada could become a legitimate enterprise if the place was appropriately organized with registered individual microentrepreneurs who held land use permits. A management committee was established to ensure compliance with a Municipal Decree (54.318/2013) that included a comprehensive set of regulations, reflecting their view on how a marketplace for low-cost goods should operate.

Despite these initiatives, illegal trade of stalls and occupation of the streets in the area persisted. In 2015, after many unsuccessful attempts to gain full control of the area, the Federal and Municipal governments agreed to concede the space to a private firm. The stated objective of this concession, similar to the construction years before, was to enhance the infrastructure of the marketplace, gain control over the space, and regulate its activities. The firm was obligated to construct a shopping center that retained the main characteristics of low-cost commerce. However, due to the high costs of rent, the shopping center has attracted little demand, and the streets continue to be populated every night by thousands of vendors.

These multiple attempts reveal that formalization has a paradoxical logic: each attempt of formalization creates requirements that exclude traders who continue to sell in stalls on the streets, where space is informally traded, as well as in other commercial buildings in the region. Thus, the ongoing existence of these low-cost garment circuits and the political patronage that sustains them have continued to depend on forbearance and extortion.

6 Conclusion: Low-Cost Fashion in Argentina and Brazil, Informality, and the Limits of the GVC Approach

In this Element, we have delved into the conditions that enabled two important circuits of low-cost garment production, distribution, and trade in Buenos Aires and São Paulo not only to endure, but also to thrive amid macroeconomic and political economic conditions that are mobilized to explain the decline of entire industries. Much has been written about the demise of the apparel industry and its jobs in traditional garment districts, like New York and London, as a result of relocation to low-wage countries. Mass fashion was presumed to be especially susceptible to collapse in the face of fierce competition, whereas niche markets of high-added value, fashionable products could capitalize on advantages of speed, flexibility, and proximity to fashions and design hubs (Doeringer and Crane 2006; Evans and Smith 2006). In addition to these pessimistic accounts, the emergence of online retail platforms connecting low-cost producers with consumers was another challenge to apparel firms and districts.

Over the past decades, Brazil and Argentina have shared significant economic trends. Both nations experienced early deindustrialization, shifting their economic focus toward resource-intensive commodities like soybeans and beef for exports and growth. Consequently, they became susceptible to the booms and busts associated with the commodity price cycle, which affected the purchasing power of their populations. Criticisms also abounded regarding the weak integration and limited contribution to global value chains, low technological intensity, and insufficient investment in research and development to boost global competitiveness. These concerns are indeed valid. Yet, it is the low-cost mass fashion segment, often deemed the most vulnerable to international competition, that has thrived in La Salada and Feira da Madrugada.

What explains this remarkable phenomenon? Why have Argentina and Brazil fostered thriving low-cost fashion circuits, and how did their primary marketplaces, La Salada and Feira da Madrugada, come into existence? Certainly, low labor costs – stemming from an abundant and skilled workforce, enriched by waves of migration – are part of the explanation. However, several other factors must be considered when comprehending La Salada and Feira da Madrugada:

1. The abundance of downstream producers, constantly engaged with traders and consumers or serving as traders themselves, facilitating the seamless coordination of supply and demand. This positioning allows for the continual monitoring of specific consumption trends.
2. The creativity that arises from this ongoing market monitoring, giving birth to a distinct form of locally tailored fast fashion, known as "Modinha" in the Brazilian context. This creativity endows them with the same advantages of "speed, flexibility, and design" associated elsewhere with high fashion niches or upgrading processes.
3. The economic booms and busts in Argentina and Brazil over the past two decades that boasted the consumption of affordable apparel. During booms, the sales of garment surged through the inclusion of new consumers from low-income social strata. During busts, more families sought cheaper garments to retain social status that consumption expresses.
4. The evolving forbearance stance of governments and politicians, transitioning from tolerance and extortion to active promotion and legitimation of the productive activities and trade occurring in La Salada and Feira da Madrugada in varying degrees of informality. Local and national state authorities have come to see these circuits as potential sources of income generation through the development of popular entrepreneurship and the promotion of consumption for the poor and lower middle classes.

In the preceding century, both Buenos Aires and Sao Paulo boasted flourishing garment industries that attracted and trained a skilled labor force. Within the circuits we analyze, garment production thrived through well-established, enduring, fragmented systems of networked production. For over a century, individuals had the opportunity to work in these workshops or embark on self-employment as producers. This entrenched production system ensured a steady supply of low-wage labor, often supplemented by waves of migrants from Andean countries. Some workers established their own workshops, capitalizing on the knowledge, resources, and connections amassed through years of work, or in the case of migrants, drawing upon their communities of origin.

These workshops, many of which specialized in specific segments of the production chain, traditionally catered to the needs of retailers. La Salada and Feira da Madrugada emerged as initiatives by certain producers and workshops aiming to enhance their profit shares selling directly to small and medium-sized resellers.

This distinction sets them apart from the typical portrayal found in most international literature about the apparel industry. Much of this literature employs the theory of global value chains to denounce the intensive, extractive, subordinate, menial, and repetitive work carried out in sweatshops in the Global South for brands headquartered in the North in search for cheap labor in the context of growing competition. Workshops in the South are often perceived merely as sites of outsourced extraction, leveraging their competitive advantage in labor costs, facilitated by the absence of regulations, to produce designs made in the North.

This approach predicts that the distribution would be made by formal and well-known retailers, brands, or supermarkets. One of the most striking features of the La Salada and Feira da Madrugada garment economies is the absence of fully formalized companies dedicated to commercializing garments. Large fashion Argentinian and Brazilian retailers, let alone foreign groups, have a limited role in these circuits.

In association with the global value chain approach, a structuralist interpretation of informality asserts the subordinate nature of the informal sector in Latin America. However, the analyzed circuits cast doubts about these drivers of informality. Indeed, several authors (Bair 2014; Hopkins and Wallerstein 1977; Brewer 2011; Portes, Castells, and Benton 1991; Portes and Walton 1981) have insisted that the decentralization of production and the process of trade globalization have promoted subordinate relations between modern capitalist enterprises and small informal enterprises located in the peripheries. Here, the informal sector is conceived as the result of formal companies seeking flexibility and aiming to reduce their labor costs. Relevant is that the latter leads companies to violate or evade labor or otherwise laws and relocate production to countries with low labor costs (Bartley 2005; Collins 2003). Therefore, instead of focusing on the informal, productive unit, this approach emphasizes "the use of labor" by modern capitalist firms: formality or informality refers to the use of labor, which means explicitly the existence (or not) of labor contracts, safety measures, or licensing (Klein and Tokman 1988).

In this context, a valid question relates to the explanatory capacity of the structuralist approach in cases where all, or at least the vast majority, of production and commercial processes take place outside formal regulations. In a context like those analyzed in this Element, no formal subcontracting firms exist. Moreover, answering this question becomes even more challenging if we consider that governments facilitate these informal economies through their lenient approach to regulatory violations.

When we look at the production units that supply garments to La Salada and Feira da Madrugada, as we did in the supply section, we see a picture altogether different from the perspective of global garment chains on the international division of labor. Those who work in these workshops do not fulfill orders from subcontractors but design and carry out the first steps of garment production. These informal, productive units are also where subcontracting to other workshops begins. The interviews in both economies reveal a landscape of production units with low-skilled labor, high levels of unpaid family work, intensive use of labor, and little differentiation between family capital goods and workshop capital goods. The same can be observed in the commercialization of garments. Here, family micro-enterprises, low qualification of workers, and intensive use of labor are expected, which in concrete terms mean traveling long distances to meet the seller-producers in the marketplaces.

Along with these features, the low-profit margins in production and distribution indicate that these economies are oriented toward subsistence rather than profit maximization (Tokman 1978). This aspect is crucial because it indicates that these are informal economic sectors for which compliance with specific regulations entails a highly disruptive increase in costs. In other words, circumventing formal processes and regulations is essential for keeping costs low and enabling the circulation of low-cost garments.

Consequently, as Ludmer (2020) argues, the circuits we analyze are better interpreted by the diagnoses of the dualistic approach represented in the PREALC (1976) studies, insofar as these marketplaces "emerged and expanded as an income-generating alternative for a large number of marginal workers, who found an income-generating alternative through the production and marketing of various products (mainly garments)" (2019, 114). Transformations such as those mentioned previously, that is, a massive migration from neighboring countries, deindustrialization, or the drastic economic crises that have affected both countries, support the classic idea of informality in Latin America, according to which results from labor markets that cannot absorb labor for those who became unemployed or migrated to the cities.

The empirical evidence on the two circuits analyzed in this study challenges the thesis that informality results from pressure from large companies that subcontract cheap labor in peripheral countries. Theoretically, thus, this Element indicates the limitations of the global garment chain approach as a paradigmatic conceptual construct to understand how the production and distribution of garments work and provides broader insights into several current debates. The explanatory factors of the economies examined in this Element are primarily national or regional but not global. The tripartite circuit described in this study – informal workshops, marketplaces, and trade networks – reveals a phenomenon with marked autonomy from the aforementioned global chains.

An important assumption in understanding garment provision as a global process is a global division of labor according to which creativity takes place in developed countries while simple, repetitive tasks are performed in developing countries. Our study shows a different picture. The workshops in the vicinity of La Salada and Feira da Madrugada not only form regional circuits of production, distribution, and trade of low-cost fashion, connecting producers with resellers that distribute it in Argentina, Brazil, and in the neighboring countries, but they also engage in autonomous and creative tasks. These tasks involve envisaging, designing, and producing low-cost fashion, referred to as "modinha," a diminutive term Brazilian producers and sellers use to describe this style tailored for individuals within the lower and middle social strata. These are veritable fashion circuits with designers, printers, tailors, distributors, salespersons, intermediaries, and promoters of the symbols and images surrounding this fashion (Giusti 2009).

As we have detailed, these circuits draw many of their characteristics from fast fashion and may occasionally find inspiration in retail offerings. However, their primary inspiration lies in popular figures from the entertainment industry: TV stars, singers, and, increasingly, internet influencers. By closely monitoring media and the market trends in La Salada and Feira da Madrugada, producers systematically experiment with dozens of models weekly, akin to the practices of the fast fashion niche, in search of successful designs.

"Modinha" represents this rapidly evolving fashion produced in La Salada and Feira da Madrugada, distributed and resold throughout Argentina and Brazil in stores, street markets, and door-to-door sales. It is fast, flexible, and easily accessible to consumers, allowing it to promptly respond to local demands and align with their preferences regarding color, fabric, and design. Consequently, "modinha" has become a preferred choice over inexpensive garments imported from Asia, owing to its ability to swiftly respond to local consumer needs while maintaining proximity and relevance.

Accounts from producers, traders, and resellers within these markets, gathered during the research that underpins this Element, challenge prevailing narratives of hopeless dress and mere necessity. Those involved in these endeavors acknowledge their role in shaping a distinct fashion niche, influencing the clothing choices of thousands in Argentina and Brazil. Producers and resellers express a genuine enthusiasm for their work within this realm, valuing the opportunities it presents, even if it means enduring extended and demanding work hours and extensive travel.

In this context, the often-criticized disconnection of Argentina and Brazil from global value chains might, in reality, be a hidden advantage. This unique situation allows local creativity and entrepreneurship to flourish, fostering a sense of pride and ownership among those contributing to these vibrant fashion circuits.

These thriving circuits rely heavily on an enduring demand for low-cost garments, a demand seemingly impervious to the cyclical economic fluctuations experienced by the Argentinian and Brazilian economies. On the one hand, economic growth resulting from soaring commodity prices in the early 2000s, coupled with real wage increases, led to poverty reduction and boosted consumption among lower-income segments of society. Clothing became a means for these groups to express their newfound social status, with governments actively encouraging the inclusion of the poor in consumer markets as a sign of limited social mobility. In Argentina, this even led to a specific social program, "Ropa para Todos" (Clothes for Everyone), driving the demand for inexpensive clothing from La Salada.

On the other, Argentina and Brazil faced profound economic crises in the early 2000s and mid-2010s, respectively. Despite the severe impact on the middle class, these crises had minimal effect on these markets. In fact, it was during the Argentine crisis that vendors initially congregated, and marketplaces for clothes emerged in the La Salada hydrothermal pools. These spaces catered to impoverished families striving to purchase affordable clothing while retaining a semblance of social status associated with their consumption. The devaluation of the peso led vendors and consumers to shift from imported goods to locally produced garments. The best performances of the La Salada marketplace, in terms of sales levels, number of visitors, and general level of economic activity, coincide with the poor performance of the formal economy. The economic crisis of 2001 is the best example of this.

Although Feira da Madrugada was already established by the time the Brazilian economic crisis hit in 2014, it similarly thrived as consumer spending power declined. In such challenging economic scenarios, consumer preferences shifted toward more affordable clothing. The proximity to consumers enabled producers to adapt their offerings. Moreover, individuals outside the labor market sought income by reselling clothes purchased from these marketplaces in their own communities.

In both countries, these circuits have developed as a function of the permanent inability of the formal sector to generate employment opportunities. The latter is also the result of economic crises that, among other things, have displaced workers and reduced the domestic market for formally produced garments. The interviews conducted in both circuits, especially in the production sector, show people previously employed in the formal sector who were generally dismissed or perceived that "being one's boss" (Milanês 2020) would bring higher profit margins and work autonomy.

The formation and development of these marketplaces would have been impossible without the passive or active involvement of the states in Argentina and Brazil. The roles taken by states, either through their policies or omissions, encompass the comparative advantages of La Salada and Feira da Madrugada. State agents, ranging from local authorities to politicians, have played pivotal roles in their development. This involvement has taken various forms, from extortion by local state agents in exchange for overlooking illicit practices such as tax evasion, irregular land use, and labor standard violations to engineering the physical spaces and legitimizing the actors within them. State agents and politicians have also acted as political intermediaries, tolerating irregularities such as using public land, unpaid taxes, and deviations from labor standards, all justified by legitimizing discourses.

Notably, La Salada and Feira da Madrugada emerged due to selective law enforcement, targeting workshops producing for large retailers with extreme working practices while tolerating those engaged in direct sales, self-employed tailoring, vending, and resale activities. This nuanced approach to law enforcement contributed significantly to the growth and sustainability of these vibrant low-cost fashion circuits. The governments of Brazil and Argentina have embraced informality and recognized the economic and political benefits it can yield, aligning with tapping into the opportunities at the bottom of the pyramid (Prahalad 2005).

While current discussions explain enforcement manipulation as an electoral strategy, this work argues that non-enforcement becomes an attractive tool when governments need to steer the social order (Dewey and Di Carlo 2022). More specifically, this means governments use non-enforcement when they want to help an economic sector and when the country's productive structure is such that non-enforcement can be implemented more effectively than other sectoral policies. This approach, which links law enforcement to the informal economy, focuses on the constellation of power and interests around enforcing regulations (Dewey, Woll, and Ronconi 2021).

For this reason, we can assert that, in this particular case, the manipulation of enforcement has worked as a true informal industrial and social policy.

However, although we are dealing with cases of state tolerance, as Portes, Castells, and Benton (1991) pointed out thirty years ago, the tolerance observed in the economies of La Salada or Feira da Madrugada is not aimed at favoring formal capitalist enterprises, probably with the ultimate goal of promoting investments or increasing tax collection. On the contrary, it is a tolerance aimed at facilitating the reproduction of the means of subsistence of a sector of the population whose chances of getting integrated into the formal labor market are unlikely. Moreover, it helps maintain lower final costs for garments, thereby enhancing the competitiveness of local production and catering to the consumption needs and desires of lower-income families, even during times of crisis. In other words, it is a mode of state intervention in which tolerance, expressed in the absence of enforcement, considerably reinforces the autonomy of this relatively informal economy as it does not promote an increase in its links with the formal sector.

Finally, recent developments in these economies and fashion markets, such as the digitization of the economy, call for further investigation to assess their long-term impacts. Although this Element emphasizes the importance and allure of the marketplace as the meeting place par excellence between producers and retailers, several technological tools now offer the possibility of remote interaction to make payments and purchases on digital platforms. One significant development is the proliferation of electronic payment methods associated with fintechs or Central Banks in Brazil and Argentina. The ubiquitous nature of electronic payments in both economies brings back to the forefront the issue of taxation, central bank regulation, and state control. These technologies, designed to streamline payments and enhance financial inclusion, may either sustain the irregularities that bolster the competitiveness of these marketplaces or, conversely, increase the transparency of economic activities occurring within them in varying degrees of informality. They offer governments a means to gauge the scale of informal activities and combat tax evasion. For example, in Brazil, the Central Bank has introduced PIX, an instant payment method, to encourage competition among banks, but it also provides valuable data on transaction volumes.

The second noteworthy development is the growing competition posed by online retail platforms functioning as virtual marketplaces, connecting consumers directly with producers. These platforms offer producers the opportunity to reach a broader consumer base, enabling consumers, in turn, to purchase affordable clothing from anywhere in the world. While these platforms have not significantly impacted La Salada and Feira da Madrugada thus far due to local consumer preferences and the presence of competitive local producers, this landscape may change. The presence of local producers and price advantages of platforms could alter the dynamics. Consumer preferences and states' responses will influence the fate of these developments. For instance, the Brazilian Federal government has sought to impose taxes on platform-based purchases of goods, particularly those imported from China. As has been pointed out (Culpepper and Thelen 2020), these platforms, for various reasons, create an alliance with users, the regulation of which can be electorally negative for those who decide to change the status quo. Something similar can be said about the payment services offered by fintechs mentioned previously. The extent to which governments are willing to demand the same conditions from, say, Mercado Pago or Tarjeta Ualá as they do from traditional banks is still a question mark.

Drawing from the documented experiences of La Salada and Feira da Madrugada, this study posits that national garment circuits in developing countries can thrive independently of global value chains producing fast fashion for budget-conscious consumers. The ingenuity demonstrated by their producers and traders, coupled with state support through policies of forbearance, legitimation, and formalization, emerges as crucial factors in fostering the success of such circuits.

References

Abreu, Marcelo de Paiva (2004). Trade Liberalization and the Political Economy of Protection in Brazil since 1987. Buenos Aires: IDB-INTAL. https://publications.iadb.org/en/publication/trade-liberalization-and-political-economy-protection-brazil.

Acemoglu, Daron. 2005. "Politics and Economics in Weak and Strong States." Journal of Monetary Economics, Political Economy and Macroeconomics 52 (7): 1199–226.

Amengual, Matthew. 2016. Politicized Enforcement in Argentina: Labor and Environmental Regulation. New York: Cambridge University Press.

Andrade, Margarida Maria de. 1991. "Bairros além-Tamanduateí: o imigrante e a fábrica no Brás, Moóca e Belenzinho." PhD Thesis in Human Geography, Universidade de São Paulo, São Paulo.

Armando, Eduardo, Ana Claudia Azevedo, Adalberto Americo Fischmann, et al. 2016. "Business Strategy and Upgrading in Global Value Chains: A Multiple Case Study in Information Technology Firms of Brazilian Origin." RAI Revista de Administração e Inovação 13(1): 40. https://doi.org/10.1016/j.rai.2016.01.002.

Aspers, Patrik. 2010a. "Using Design for Upgrading in the Fashion Industry." Journal of Economic Geography 10(2): 189–207.

Aspers, Patrik. 2010b. Orderly Fashion: A Sociology of Markets. Princeton: Princeton University Press.

Bair, Jennifer. 2009. Frontiers of Commodity Chain Research. California: Stanford University Press.

Bair, Jennifer. 2014. "Editors Introduction: Commodity Chains in and of the World System." Journal of World-Systems Research 20(1): 1–10.

Bair, Jennifer, and Marion Werner. 2011. "Commodity Chains and the Uneven Geographies of Global Capitalism: A Disarticulations Perspective." Environment and Planning A 43(5): 988–97.

Bartley, Tim. 2005. "Corporate Accountability and the Privatization of Labor Standards: Struggles over Codes of Conduct in the Apparel Industry." Research in Political Sociology 14: 211–244.

BCB (Banco Central do Brasil). 2020. Lançamento da marca PIX. Recorded press conference. February 19, 2020. www.youtube.com/watch?v=grX3'av81FJA&list=PLhqfgkxuHXh7A_K7cQXOsK9sNVVToun2b&index=121. Accessed on July 5, 2023.

BCRA (Banco Central de la República Argentina). 2022. Sistema Nacional de Pagos. Resoluciones A 7510, 7533, 7585 y 7495.

Beckert, Jens, and Patrik Aspers. 2011. The Worth of Goods: Valuation and Pricing in the Economy. Oxford: Oxford University Press.

Benencia, Roberto, and Santiago Canevaro. 2017. "Migración boliviana y negocios. De la discriminación a la aceptación. La Salada como fenómeno social." REMHU: Revista Interdisciplinar da Mobilidade Humana 25(49): 175–96.

Benencia, Roberto Rodolfo, and German Jorge Quaranta. 2006. Mercados de trabajo y economías de enclave: La "escalera boliviana" en la actualidad. Estudios migratorios Latinoamericanos 20(60): 413–22.

Besley, Timothy, and Torsten Persson. 2009. "The Origins of State Capacity: Property Rights, Taxation, and Politics." American Economic Review 99(4): 1218–44.

Blumer, Herbert. 1969. "Fashion: From Class Differentiation to Collective Selection." The Sociological Quarterly 10(3): 275–91. https://10.1111/j.1533-8525.1969.tb01292.x.

Bobbio, Emmanuele. 2016. "Tax Evasion, Firm Dynamics and Growth." SSRN Scholarly Paper. Rochester, NY. https://doi.org/10.2139/ssrn.2910376.

Bonacich, Edna, and Richard Appelbaum. 2000. Behind the Label: Inequality in the Los Angeles Apparel Industry. London: University of California Press.

Boon, Marcus. 2010. In Praise of Copying. Cambridge, Massachusetts: Harvard University Press.

Boudreau, Julie-Anne, and Diane E Davis. 2017. "Introduction: A Processual Approach to Informalization." Current Sociology 65(2): 151–66.

Brewer, Benjamin D. 2011. "Global Commodity Chains & World Income Inequalities: The Missing Link of Inequality and the Upgrading Paradox." Journal of World-Systems Research, August, 17(2): 308–27.

Bromley, Raymond J., and Richard Symanski. 1974. "Marketplace Trade in Latin America." Latin American Research Review 9(3): 3–38.

Calíope, Thalita Silva, and José Carlos Lázaro da Silva Filho. 2019. NA Feira Também Tem Inovação? Uma análise Da Criação E Confecção de "Modinha" NA Feira Da Rua José Avelino. Gestão & Regionalidade 35(105): 142–60. https://doi.org/10.13037/gr.vol35n105.5088.

Ceccagno, Antonella. 2017. City Making and Global Labor Regimes: Chinese Immigrants and Italy's Fast Fashion Industry. Cham, Switzerland: Palgrave Macmillan.

Ceccagno, Antonella. 2024. "Selective Law Enforcement at the Intersection of Ethnicity and Entrepreneurship." Journal of Ethnic and Migration Studies 50(8): 2078–2096.

Chu, Nellie. 2016. "The Emergence of 'Craft' and Migrant Entrepreneurship along the Global Commodity Chains for Fast Fashion in Southern China." The Journal of Modern Craft 9(2): 193–213.

Cochoy, Franck. 2007. "A Sociology of Market-Things: On Tending the Garden of Choices in Mass Retailing". The Sociological Review 55(2_suppl): 109–29. https://doi.org/10.1111/j.1467-954X.2007.00732.x.

Collins, Jane Lou. 2003. Threads: Gender, Labor, and Power in the Global Apparel Industry. Chicago: University of Chicago Press.

Coombe, Rosemary J. 1993. "Tactics of Appropriation and the Politics of Recognition in Late Modern Democracies." Political Theory 21(3): 411–33.

Crofton, Stephanie, and Luis Dopico. 2007. "Zara-Inditex and the Growth of Fast Fashion." *Essays in Economic & Business History* 25: 41–54.

Culpepper, Pepper. D., and Thelen, Kathleen. 2020. "Are We All Amazon Primed? Consumers and the Politics of Platform Power." Comparative Political Studies 53(2): 288–318. https://doi.org/10.1177/0010414019852687.

D'Angiolillo, Julián, Marcelo Dimentstein, Martín Di Peco, et al. 2010. "Feria La Salada: Una centralidad periférica intermitente en el Gran Buenos Aires." In Argentina: persistencia y diversificación, contrastes e imaginarios en las centralidades urbanas, edited by Margarita Gutman and Fernando Carrión, 169–206. Quito: Olacchi.

Davis, Diane E. 2017. "Informality and State Theory: Some Concluding Remarks." Current Sociology 65(2): 315–24.

Dewey, Matías. 2017. "State-Sponsored Protection Rackets. Regulating the Market for Counterfeit Clothing in Argentina." In The Architecture of Illegal Markets: Towards an Economic Sociology of Illegality in the Economy, edited by Jens Beckert and Matías Dewey, 123–40. Oxford: Oxford University Press.

Dewey, Matías. 2018a. "Domestic Obstacles to Labor Standards: Law Enforcement and Informal Institutions in Argentina's Garment Industry." Socio-Economic Review 16(3): 567–86. https://doi.org/10.1093/ser/mwx028.

Dewey, Matías. 2018b. "The Other Taxation: An Ethnographic Account of 'Off-the-Books' State Financing." Latin American Research Review 53(4): 726–40.

Dewey, Matías. 2020a. Making It at Any Cost: Apirations and Politics in a Counterfeit Clothing Marketplace. Austin: University of Texas Press.

Dewey, Matías. 2020b. "The Creative Copy: Agency and Fashion at a Market for Counterfeited Garments." In Piracy and Intellectual Property in Latin America: Rethinking Creativity and the Common Good, edited by Goldgel

Carballo, Víctor, and Juan Poblete, 191–206. New York: Routledge. https://public.ebookcentral.proquest.com/choice/publicfullrecord.aspx?p=6126604.

Dewey, Matías. 2022. "La Economía de La Salada En Tiempos de Pandemia: Concentración Productiva, Tecnologías Digitales y Erosión Del Poder Estatal." In La Democracia Ante La Pandemia. Transformaciones Interamericanas, edited by Armin von Bogdandy, Andrés Malamud, and Mariela Morales Antoniazzi, 325–46. Buenos Aires: Katz Editores.

Dewey, Matías, and Donato Di Carlo. 2022. "Governing through Non-Enforcement: Regulatory Forbearance as Industrial Policy in Advanced Economies." Regulation & Governance 16(3): 930–50.

Dewey, Matías, Cornelia Woll, Lucas Ronconi. 2021. The Political Economy of Law Enforcement, MaxPo Discussion Paper, No. 21/1, Max Planck Sciences Po Center on Coping with Instability in Market Societies (MaxPo), Paris

DOCSP. 2006. "Combate ao comércio irregular cria novas oportunidades de trabalho." Diário Oficial da Cidade de São Paulo, p. I, February 14, 2006.

DOCSP. 2007. "Prefeitura inicia operação noturna contra comércio irregular no Brás." Diário Oficial da Cidade de São Paulo, p. II, August 21, 2007.

DOCSP. 2008a. Mr. Adilson Amadeu's Speech at the 312nd São Paulo Town Hall's Ordinary Session, November 22, 2007. Diário Oficial da Cidade de São Paulo, p. 118, March 1, 2008.

DOCSP. 2008b. Mr. Jose Americo's Speech (as the Workers Party leader) at the 312nd São Paulo Town Hall's Ordinary Session, November 22nd, 2007. Diário Oficial da Cidade de São Paulo, p. 118, March 1, 2008.

DOCSP. 2008c. Mr. Paulo Fiorilo's Speech at the 377th São Paulo Town Hall's Ordinary Session, August 6th, 2008. Diário Oficial da Cidade de São Paulo, p. 97, December 13, 2008.

Doeringer, Peter, and Sarah Crean. 2006. "Can Fast Fashion Save the US Apparel Industry?" Socio-Economic Review 4(3): 353–77. https://doi.org/10.1093/ser/mwl014.

ESTADO de São Paulo. 2012. "Propina amplia feira 'sem lei' da madrugada, em SP." Estado de Sao Paulo, November 29, 2012. www.estadao.com.br/noticias/geral,propina-amplia-feira-sem-lei-da-madrugada-em-sp,966846. Accessed on July 16, 2023.

Evans, Yara, and Adrian Smith. 2006. "Surviving at the Margins? Deindustrialisation, the Creative Industries, and Upgrading in London's Garment Sector." Environment and Planning A 38(12): 2253–69.

de la Feria, Rita. 2020. "Tax Fraud and Selective Law Enforcement." Journal of Law and Society 47: 240–270.

Ferreira, Francisco H. G., Julian Messina, Jamele Rigolini, et al. 2013. Economic Mobility and the Rise of the Latin American Middle Class. Washington, DC: The World Bank.

Folha de S. Paulo. 2003a. "'Feirinha da madrugada' surge no Brás." August 7, 2003. Accessed on January 24, 2023. https://www1.folha.uol.com.br/fsp/cotidian/ff0708200304.htm.

Folha de S. Paulo. 2003b. "Comerciante cobra ação contra feira illegal." August 07, 2003. Accessed on January 24, 2023. https://www1.folha.uol.com.br/fsp/cotidian/ff0708200303.htm.

FOLHA de São Paulo. 2019. RUF 2019: Ranking Universitário Folha. https://ruf.folha.uol.com.br/2019/ranking-de-cursos/moda/. Accessed on July 16, 2023.

Forment, Carlos A. 2015. "Ordinary Ethics and the Emergence of Plebeian Democracy across the Global South: Buenos Aires's La Salada Market." Current Anthropology 56(11): 116–125.

G1. 2008. "Polícia prende suspeitos de integrar nova máfia dos fiscais em SP." July 11, 2008. http://g1.globo.com/Noticias/SaoPaulo/0,,MUL643486-5605,00-POLICIA+PRENDE+SUSPEITOS+DE+INTEGRAR+NOVA+MAFIA+DOS+FISCAIS+EM+SP.html. Accessed on November 25, 2022.

Gago, Verónica. 2012. "La Salada: ¿un caso de globalización «desde abajo»?" Nueva Sociedad 241: 63–78.

Garcia, Marie-France. 1986." La Construction Sociale d'un marché parfait: le marché au cadran de Fontaines en Sologne." Actes de la Recherche en Sciences Sociales, 65: 2–13.

Geertz, Clifford, Hildred Geertz, and Lawrence Rosen. 1979. Meaning and Order in Moroccan Society: Three Essays in Cultural Analysis. Cambridge, MA: Cambridge University Press.

Genschel, Philipp, and Peter Schwarz. 2011. "Tax Competition: A Literature Review." Socio-Economic Review 9(2): 339–70.

Gereffi, Gary, David Spener, and Jennifer Bair. 2002. Free Trade and Uneven Development: The North American Apparel Industry after NAFTA. Philadelphia: Temple University Press.

Gereffi, Gary, and Miguel Korzeniewicz, eds. 1994. Commodity Chains and Global Capitalism. Westport, CO: Praeger.

Gereffi, Gary, and Olga Memedovic. 2003. "The Global Apparel Value Chain. What Prospects for Upgrading by Developing Countries?" Vienna: United Nations Industrial Development, p. 36

Gerring, John. 2006. Case Study Research: Principles and Practices. Cambridge: Cambridge University Press.

Giusti, Nicoletta. 2009. Introduzione allo studio della moda. Milano: Il Mulino.

Gordon, Sanford C., and Catherine Hafer. 2013. "Conditional Forbearance as an Alternative to Capture." In Preventing Regulatory Capture: Special Interest Influence and How to Limit It, edited by Daniel Carpenter and David A. Moss, 208–38. Cambridge: Cambridge University Press.

Green, Nancy. 1997. Ready-to-Wear, Ready-to-Work: A Century of Industry and Immigrants in Paris and New York. Durham: Duke University Press.

Guha-Khasnobis, Basudeb, S. M. Ravi Kanbur, and Elinor Ostrom, eds. 2006. Linking the Formal and Informal Economy: Concepts and Policies. UNU-WIDER Studies in Development Economics. Oxford: Oxford University Press.

Haddad, Beatriz Sumaya Malavasi & Castro, Ana Lucia de. 2019. "'Moda, eu faço a minha': a circulação de símbolos globais de moda entre grupos de baixa renda." Contemporânea: Revista de Sociologia da UFSCar 9(1): 229–52.

Hiratuka, Célio & Renato de Castro Garcia. 1995. Impactos da abertura comercial sobre a dinâmica da indústria têxtil brasileira. Leituras de Economia Política 1(1): 1–21.

Holland, Alisha C. 2016. "Forbearance." American Political Science Review 110(2): 232–46.

Holland, Alisha C. 2017. Forbearance as Redistribution: The Politics of Informal Welfare in Latin America. Cambridge: Cambridge University Press.

Hopkins, Terence K., and Immanuel Wallerstein. 1977. "Patterns of Development of the Modern World-System." Review (Fernand Braudel Center), 1(2): 111–45.

Hu, Allison. 2012. "Fair Game: Learning from La Salada." BA thesis, Massachusetts Institute of Technology.

Infobae. 2017. CAME: aumentó la venta ilegal a nivel nacional. June 12, 2017. www.infobae.com/economia/2017/06/12/came-aumento-la-venta-ilegal-a-nivel-nacional/.

Kawamura, Yuniya. 2005. Fashion-Ology: An Introduction to Fashion Studies. Oxford: Berg.

Kerstenetzky, Celia, Christiane Uchôa, & Nelson do Valle Silva. 2015. The Elusive New Middle Class in Brazil. Brazilian Political Science Review 9(3): 21–41.

Kim, Jihye. 2021. From Sweatshop to Fashion Shop: Korean Immigrant Entrepreneurship in the Argentine Garment Industry. Korean Communities across the World. Lanham: Lexington Books.

Klein, Emilio, and Víctor E. Tokman. 1988. "Sector Informal: Una Forma de Utilizar El Trabajo Como Consecuencia de La Manera de Producir y No

Viceversa. A Propósito Del Artículo de Portes y Benton." Estudios Sociológicos 6(16): 205–12.

Kopper, Moisés & Arlei Sander Damo. 2018. "A emergência e evanescência da nova classe média brasileira." Horizontes Antropológicos 24(50): 335–76.

Kosacoff, Bernardo, Guillermo Anlló, Carlos Bianco, et al. 2004. "Evaluación de Un Escenario Posible y Deseable de Reestructuración y Fortalecimiento Del Complejo Textil Argentino." Cepal-Oficina de Buenos Aires (LC/BUE/ R. 261), Octubre. www.cepal.org/publicaciones/Buenosaires/1/ LCBUER261/textiles.pdf.

Lempert, Michael. 2014. "Imitation." Annual Review of Anthropology 43(1): 379–95.

Ludmer, Gustavo. 2020. "Análisis de las causas de la informalidad laboral en la industria de confección de indumentaria. Argentina : 1975–2018," March. http://ridaa.unq.edu.ar/handle/20.500.11807/3599.

Luvaas, Brent. 2013. "Material Interventions : Indonesian DIY Fashion and the Regime of the Global Brand." Cultural Anthropology 28(1): 127–43.

MacKenzie, Donald A. 2009. Material Markets: How Economic Agents Are Constructed. Clarendon Lectures in Management Studies. Oxford; New York: Oxford University Press.

Magalhães, Vera. 2011. "Folha de S.Paulo - PR fez 'rolo compressor', diz empresário." July 23, 2011. Accessed on January 24, 2023. https://www1 .folha.uol.com.br/fsp/poder/po2307201107.htm.

Manning, Paul. 2010. "The Semiotics of Brand." Annual Review of Anthropology 39(1): 33–49.

Meagher, Kate. 2013. "Unlocking the Informal Economy: A Literature Review on Linkages between Formal and Informal Economies in Developing Countries." Work. EPap 27.

Meagher, Kate. 2016. "Capitalizing on Informality: Varieties of Actually Existing Informal Economies in Africa." Proceedings of the African Futures Conference 1(1): 159. https://doi.org/10.1002/j.2573-508X.2016 .tb00044.x.

Milanês, Renata. 2020. "O trabalho das mulheres costureiras na zona rural do Agreste pernambucano." IDeAS 14(1): 9.

Milanés, Renata. 2024. "Starting a Business Here is Very Easy": Creative Practices and Entrepreneurial Bricolage in a Brazilian Clothing Market. Unpublished Manuscript.

Milmanda, Belén Fernández, and Candelaria Garay. 2019. "The Multilevel Politics of Enforcement: Environmental Institutions in Argentina." Politics & Society 48(1): 3–26.

Misse, Michel. 2010. Trocas ilícitas e mercadorias políticas: para uma interpretação de trocas ilícitas e moralmente reprováveis cuja persistência e abrangência no Brasil nos causam incômodos também teóricos. Anuário Antropológico 35(2): 89–107.

Monteiro Filha, Dulce Corrêa and Abidack Raposo Correa. 2002. O complexo têxtil In São Paulo, Elizabeth Maria de; Jorge Kalache Filho (orgs.). Banco Nacional de Desenvolvimento Econômico e Social 50 anos: histórias setoriais, 241–73. Rio de Janeiro: DBA.

Nakassis, Constantine V. 2012. "Counterfeiting What? Aesthetics of Brandedness and BRAND in Tamil Nadu, India." Anthropological Quarterly 85(3): 701–21.

Neri, Marcelo. 2011. A nova classe média: o lado brilhante da base da pirâmide. São Paulo: Saraiva.

O'Dougherty, Maureen. 1998. "Auto-Retratos da Classe Média: Hierarquias de 'Cultura' e Consumo em São Paulo." Dados 41(2): 411–44.

OECD, ITC. 2015. "Examples of Successful DRM Reforms and the Role of International Co-Operation." Discussion Paper.

Ojeda, Igor. 2014. Zara admite que houve escravidão na produção de suas roupas em 2011. *Repórter Brasil.* https://reporterbrasil.org.br/2014/05/zara-admite-que-houve-escravidao-na-producao-de-suas-roupas-em-2011/. Accessed on July 5, 2023.

Olivera, Francisco. 2023. Ecos de la derrota peronista: postergan la feria pensada para competir con La Salada. *La Nación*, December 6, 2023. www.lanacion.com.ar/economia/ecos-de-la-derrota-peronista-postergan-la-feria-pensada-para-competir-con-la-salada-nid06122023/. Accessed on July 1, 2024.

Pardo-Guerra, Juan Pablo. 2019. Automating Finance: Infrastructures, Engineers, and the Making of Electronic Markets. Cambridge, United Kingdom: Cambridge University Press.

Piore, Michael J., & Sabel, Charles F. 1984. The Second Industrial Divide: Possibilities for Prosperity. New York: Basic Books.

Piore, Michael, and Cauam Ferreira Cardoso. 2019. "Beyond the Silicon Valley Consensus: Understanding the Organizational Challenges and Opportunities for Promoting Innovation in Brazil." In Innovation in Brazil: Advancing Development in the 21st Century, edited by Elisabeth B. Reynolds, Ben Ross Schneider & Ezequiel Zylberberg, 211–30. London: Routledge.

Pogliaghi, Leticia. 2008. "Informalidad urbana. Una aproximación a partir de un estudio de caso: las ferias de La Salada, Lomas de Zamora (2006–2007)." MA thesis, Universidad Nacional de General San Martín, Buenos Aires.

Portes, Alejandro, and John Walton. 1981. Labor, Class, and the International System: Studies in Social Discontinuity. New York: Academic Press.

Portes, Alejandro, Manuel Castells, and Lauren Benton. 1991. The Informal Economy: Studies in Advanced and Less Developed Countries. Baltimore, MD: Johns Hopkins University Press.

Prahalad, Coimbatore K. 2005. The Fortune at the Bottom of the Pyramid. Upper Saddle River, NJ [Harlow]: Wharton School Publishing.

PREALC (Programa Regional del Empleo para América Latina y el Caribe). 1976. El problema del empleo en América Latina: Situación, perspectivas y políticas. Santiago de Chile: PREALC.

Raustiala, Kal, and Christopher Sprigman. 2012. The Knockoff Economy. How Imitation Sparks Innovation. Oxford: Oxford University Press.

Ronconi, Lucas. 2012. "Globalization, Domestic Institutions, and Enforcement of Labor Law: Evidence from Latin America." Industrial Relations: A Journal of Economy and Society 51(1): 89–105.

Rooij, Benjamin Van, Gerald E. Fryxell, Carlos Wing-Hung Lo, and Wei Wang. 2013. "From Support to Pressure: The Dynamics of Social and Governmental Influences on Environmental Law Enforcement in Guangzhou City, China." Regulation & Governance 7(3): 321–47.

Rougier, Marcelo, and Graciela Pampin. 2015. "Orígenes y Esplendor de La Industria En El Gran Buenos Aires." In Historia de La Provincia de Buenos Aires: El Gran Buenos Aires, edited by Gabriel Kessler, 6:195–224. Buenos Aires: unipe – edhasa.

Santiago, Igor Mauler. 2010. "Free Competition: How Tax Evasion and Tax Competition Distort Markets; The Brazilian Perspective." Intertax 38(3): 170–76. https://kluwerlawonline.com/api/Product/CitationPDFURL?file=Journals\TAXI\TAXI2010019.pdf.

Sassen, Saskia. 2011. "La Salada: The Largest Informal Market in South America." Forbes. Accessed November 4, 2024. La Salada: The Largest Informal Market in South America .

Scalon, Celi, and André Salata. 2012. "Uma nova classe média no Brasil da última década? O debate a partir da perspectiva sociológica." Sociedade e Estado 27(2): 387–407.

Scott, James C. 1998. Seeing like a State How Certain Schemes to Improve the Human Condition Have Failed. New Haven: Yale University Press.

Silva, Carlos Freire da. 2014. "Das calçadas às galerias: mercados populares do centro de São Paulo." Text, Universidade de São Paulo. https://doi.org/10.11606/T.8.2014.tde-31032015-105012.

Silva, Sydney A. da. 2012. Bolivianos em São Paulo. Dinâmica cultural e processos identitários. In Imigração Boliviana no Brasil, edited by Rosana Baeninger,

19–34. Campinas: Núcleo de Estudos de População-Nepo/Unicamp; Fapesp; CNPq; Unfpa.

Souza, Jessé de. 2010. Os batalhadores brasileiros: nova classe média ou nova classe trabalhadora? Belo Horizonte: Editora UFMG.

Tavosnanska, Andrés, ed. 2010. "La Industria Argentina En El Ciclo 2003–2008. Nuevas Dinámicas, Nuevos Actores, Perspectivas." http://home.econ .uba.ar/economicas/sites/default/files/cespa23.pdf.

Tokatli, Nebahat. 2007. "Networks, Firms and Upgrading within the Blue-Jeans Industry: Evidence from Turkey." Global Networks 7(1): 51–68.

Tokatli, Nebahat. 2013. "Toward a Better Understanding of the Apparel Industry: A Critique of the Upgrading Literature." Journal of Economic Geography 13(6): 993–1011.

Tokman, Victor E. 1978. "An Exploration into the Nature of Informal-Formal Sector Relationships." World Development 6 (9/10): 1065–75.

Tokman, Victor E., ed. 1992. Beyond Regulation: The Informal Economy in Latin America. Boulder: Lynne Rienner Publishers .

Vereta-Nahoum, André. 2019. "The Making of a Proper Marketplace: The Politics of Infrastructure in the Night Market (São Paulo)." In The Political and Cultural Economy of Popular Commerce: Gender, Inequality, and Materiality in Latin American Cities, edited by Eveline Dürr and Juliane Müller, 87–108. London: Lexington.

Vereta-Nahoum, André. 2021. Tecendo um Circuito Comercial a Partir Da Feira Da Madrugada as Agenciadoras Da Moda Popular Brasileira. Revista Brasileira de Ciências Sociais, 36(105): 1–25.

Vio, Marcelo, and María C. Cabrera. 2015. "Panorámicas de La Producción En El Conurbano Reciente." In Historia de La Provincia de Buenos Aires: El Gran Buenos Aires, edited by Gabriel Kessler, 255–85. Buenos Aires: unipe – edhasa.

Weber, Max. 1978. Economy and Society: An Outline of Interpretive Sociology. Vol. I. Berkeley: University of California Press.

Williams, Colin. 2017. Entrepreneurship in the Informal Sector: An Institutional Perspective. New York: Routledge.

Yaccoub, Hilaine. 2011. "A Chamada 'Nova Classe Média': Cultura Material, Inclusão E Distinção Social." Horizontes Antropológicos, 17(36): 197–231.

Zaloom, Caitlin. 2006. Out of the Pits. Chicago: Chicago University Press.

Cambridge Elements ☰

Politics and Society in Latin America

Maria Victoria Murillo

Columbia University

Maria Victoria Murillo is Professor of Political Science and International Affairs at Columbia University. She is the author of Political Competition, Partisanship, and Policymaking in the Reform of Latin American Public Utilities (Cambridge, 2009). She is also editor of Carreras Magisteriales, Desempeño Educativo y Sindicatos de Maestros en América Latina (2003), and co-editor of *Argentine Democracy: The Politics of Institutional Weakness* (2005). She has published in edited volumes as well as in the *American Journal of Political Science, World Politics*, and *Comparative Political Studies*, among others.

Juan Pablo Luna

The Pontifical Catholic University of Chile

Juan Pablo Luna is Professor of Political Science at Pontificia Universidad Católica de Chile. He received his BA in Applied Social Sciences from the UCUDAL (Uruguay) and his PhD in Political Science from the University of North Carolina at Chapel Hill. He is the author of *Segmented Representation. Political Party Strategies in Unequal Democracies* (Oxford University Press, 2014), and has co-authored *Latin American Party Systems* (Cambridge University Press, 2010). In 2014, along with Cristobal Rovira, he co-edited *The Resilience of the Latin American Right* (Johns Hopkins University). His work on political representation, state capacity, and organized crime has appeared in the following journals: *Comparative Political Studies, Revista de Ciencia Política, the Journal of Latin American Studies, Latin American Politics and Society, Studies in Comparative International Development, Política y Gobierno, Democratization, Perfiles Latinoamericanos*, and the *Journal of Democracy.*

Andrew Schrank

Brown University

Andrew Schrank is the Olive C. Watson Professor of Sociology and International & Public Affairs at Brown University. His articles on business, labor, and the state in Latin America have appeared in the *American Journal of Sociology, Comparative Politics, Comparative Political Studies, Latin American Politics & Society, Social Forces*, and *World Development*, among other journals, and his co-authored book, *Root-Cause Regulation: Labor Inspection in Europe and the Americas*, is forthcoming at Harvard University Press.

Advisory Board

Javier Auyero, *University of Texas at Austin*

Daniela Campello, *Fundação Getúlio Vargas*

Eduardo Dargent, *Universidad Catolica, Peru*

Alberto Diaz-Cayeros, *Stanford University*

Kathy Hoschtetler, *London School of Economics*

Evelyne Huber, *University of North Carolina, Chapel Hill*

Robert Kaufman, *Rutgers University*

Steven Levitsky, *Harvard University*

Antonio Lucero, *University of Washington, Seattle*

Juliana Martinez, *Universidad de Costa Rica*

Alfred P. Montero, *Carlton College*
Alison Post, *University of California, Berkeley*
Gabriel Vommaro, *Universidad Nacional de General Sarmiento*
Deborah Yashar, *Princeton University*
Gisela Zaremberg, *Flacso México*
Veronica Zubilaga, *Universidad Simon Bolivar*

About the Series

Latin American politics and society are at a crossroads, simultaneously confronting serious challenges and remarkable opportunities that are likely to be shaped by formal institutions and informal practices alike. The Elements series on Politics and Society in Latin America offers multidisciplinary and methodologically pluralist contributions on the most important topics and problems confronted by the region.

Cambridge Elements ᐦ

Politics and Society in Latin America

Elements in the Series

The Distributive Politics of Environmental Protection in Latin America and the Caribbean
Isabella Alcañiz, Ricardo A. Gutiérrez

The Circuit of Detachment in Chile
Kathya Araujo

Beyond 'Plata O Plomo'
Gustavo Duncan

The Post-Partisans
Carlos Meléndez

The Political Economy of Segmented Expansion:Latin American Social Policy in the 2000s
Camila Arza, Rossana Castiglioni, Juliana Martínez Franzoni, Sara Niedzwiecki, Jennifer Pribble, Diego Sánchez-Ancochea

Feminisms in Latin America: Pro-choice Nested Networks in Mexico and Brazil
Gisela Zaremberg, Débora Rezende de Almeida

Innovating Democracy? The Means and Ends of Citizen Participation in Latin America
Thamy Pogrebinschi

The Indigenous Right to Self-Determination in Extractivist Economies
Marcela Torres-Wong

Conservatives against the Tide: The Rise of the Argentine PRO in Comparative Perspective
Gabriel Vommaro

Costly Opportunities
María José Álvarez-Rivadulla

Parties and New Technologies in Latin America
Rafael Piñeiro-Rodríguez, Fernando Rosenblatt, Gabriel Vommaro, and Laura Wills-Otero

Low-Cost Fashion: The Political Economy of Garment Production and Distribution in Latin America
Matías Dewey and André-Vereta-Nahoum

A full series listing is available at: www.cambridge.org/PSLT

www.ingramcontent.com/pod-product-compliance
Ingram Content Group UK Ltd.
Pitfield, Milton Keynes, MK11 3LW, UK
UKHW030736130225
454942UK00026B/644

9 781009 634151